Connections: Key Themes in World History

TRADING TASTES

Commodity and Culture Exchange to 1750

Erik Gilbert
Arkansas State University

Jonathan T. Reynolds
Northern Kentucky University

PEARSON

Prentice Hall

Upper Saddle River, New Jersey 07458

Library of Congress Cataloging-in-Publication Data

Gilbert, Erik.
  Trading tastes : commodity and culture exchange to 1750 / Erik Gilbert, Jonathan T. Reynolds.
    p. cm.
  Includes bibliographical references and index.
  1. Commerce—History. 2. Commercial products—History. 3. International
trade—History. 4. Cultural relations—History. I. Reynolds, Jonathan T. II. Title.

  HF352.G55 2006
  382'.456645—dc22

2005020881

VP, Editorial Director: Charlyce Jones Owen
Executive Editor: Charles Cavaliere
Editorial Assistant: Maria Guarascio
Executive Marketing Manager: Heather Shelstad
Marketing Assistant: Jennifer Lang
Sr. Managing Editor: Joanne Riker
Production Liaison: Jan H. Schwartz
Buyer: Ben Smith
Cover Designer: Bruce Kenselaar
Cover Art: Ports, islands, and cities on the African and Indian coast, Courtesy of the Library
  of Congress
Director, Image Resource Center: Melinda Reo
Manager, Rights and Permissions: Zina Arabia
Manager, Visual Research: Beth Brenzel
Manager, Cover Visual Research and Permissions: Karen Sanatar
Composition/Full-Service Management: Integra, Kalpalathika Rajan
Printer/Binder: Courier Stoughton, Inc.
Cover Printer: Courier Stoughton, Inc.

Credits and acknowledgements borrowed from other sources and reproduced, with permission, in this textbook appear on appropriate page within text.

Pearson Education LTD.
Pearson Education Singapore, Pte. Ltd
Pearson Education Canada, Ltd
Pearson Education—Japan

Pearson Education Australia PTY, Limited
Pearson Education North Asia Ltd
Pearson Educación de Mexico, S.A. de C.V.
Pearson Education Malaysia, Pte. Ltd

10 9 8 7 6 5 4 3 2 1
ISBN 0-13-190007-2

For our siblings:
Glenn, Katy, Brad, Chris and Peter

Contents

Foreword

Connections: Key Themes in World History focuses on specific issues of world historical significance from antiquity to the present by employing a combination of explanatory narrative, primary sources, questions relating to those sources, a summary analysis, and further points to ponder, all of which combine to enable readers to discover some of the most important driving forces in world history.

The increasingly rapid pace and specialization of historical inquiry has created an ever-widening gap between professional publications and general surveys, especially surveys of world history. The purpose of *Connections* is to bridge that gap by placing the latest research and debates on selected topics of global historical significance, as well as some of the evidence upon which historians base their insights, into a form and context that is comprehensible to students and general readers alike.

Two pedagogical principles infuse this series. First, students master world history most easily if allowed to focus on specific themes and issues. Such themes, by their very specificity, as well as because of their general application, enable students to perceive and understand more clearly than is possible through reading, by itself, a massive world history textbook, the overall patterns and meaning of our shared global past. Second, students learn best when asked to think critically about what they are studying. So far as the study of history is concerned, critical thinking necessarily involves analysis of primary sources.

To that end, we offer a series of brief, tightly focused books that embrace a radical simplicity and a provocative format. Each book goes to the heart of a key theme, phenomenon, or issue in world history—something that has connected humans across cultures, continents, and time spans. By actively engaging with this material, the reader comes to understand in a nuanced and meaningful manner how often distantly located human cultures have been connected to one another as key actors in the epic story of world history.

Alfred J. Andrea
Professor Emeritus of History
University of Vermont

Series Editor's Preface

Trade and commerce have been primary forces in the dynamics of world history since before the dawn of agriculture. For better and for worse, trade has been a major factor in the transmission of foreign products, ideas, belief systems, modes of artistic expression, and even flora and fauna to far-away host cultures. The existence of a seal from the ancient Indus Valley civilization known to us as Harappan, which dates to circa 2100–1750 B.C.E., showing four human figures somersaulting forward and backward over the raised horns of a bull, brings to mind the somewhat later images of bull-leapers from the island civilization of Minoan Crete, over 3,000 miles away. A wealth of documentary evidence shows beyond any doubt that a lively trade in goods connected Mesopotamia with the Indus Valley to its southeast and the region to its west that stretches from Anatolia (modern Asiatic Turkey) to Egypt. Yet, we can only speculate about the specific trade connections that transmitted the image and idea of bull leaping up the Persian Gulf, through Mesopotamia, Anatolia, and Syria-Palestine, and into the wine-dark waters of the Mediterranean. We can also only speculate how many merchants might have been involved in that transit of commodities and ideas. Indeed, almost all the traders of antiquity are anonymous to us, and the same is true of the vast majority of merchants from more recent centuries. Likewise, many of the ancient trade routes are lost or little understood today, and many of the more recent trade routes are still hazy to us. Notwithstanding, as the authors of this little book so aptly illustrate, we know quite a bit about the general patterns and significance of trans-continental and trans-oceanic trade from antiquity to the present, and it is those patterns and impact that this book examines through its analysis of the production and long-distance trade of four commodities: spice (or spices), salt, sugar, and silk from ancient times to about 1750 C.E., the putative starting point of the Modern Era.

Gilbert and Reynolds have chosen these four trade items not out of a love of alliteration (although their lively prose style indulges at times in irreverent asides and humorous figures of speech) but because individually and collectively the four items are excellent case studies. Individually, spice, salt, sugar, and silk are prisms through which we can view the diverse ways in which commodity production and long-distance trade have influenced the historical development of cultures, societies, human relationships, and states, as well as economies. Collectively, the four show us how over the course of more than a millennium and a half long-distance trade in high-value, low-bulk, essentially unnecessary, "splendid, trifling things" for the elite few metamorphosed into a global commerce in high-bulk, moderately low-value goods that are significantly more necessary to human life and the general comfort of all members of society. Several of the commodities featured here, notably salt and sugar, also demonstrate how notions of value change over time in response to the globalization of commerce and the industrialization of production. Items that were once rare or difficult to obtain, and therefore precious, have become commonplace and inexpensive.

Beyond that, the authors demonstrate in their prose narratives and in the primary sources that they have selected for the reader's analysis, that until the fairly recent revolution in long-distance communication that began not much more than a century and a half ago, trade was probably the single most important vehicle, arguably more important even than imperial expansion, for disseminating ideas and other cultural elements from one people to another. The processes of transmission were complex and varied, but several general patterns are easily comprehended. First, merchants and those who traveled with them constituted probably the single most important cohort of cultural carriers in the history of the world—at least until fairly recent times. Second, the cultural influences they transmitted into foreign environments were not simply adopted; they were adapted to the hosts' preexisting cultures. We term this process of adaptive absorption "syncretism." Third, very much like the economic exchange in whose wake it followed, cultural transmission was, more precisely, cultural exchange. Caravan routes and shipping lanes were two-way avenues, and cultural influences flowed both ways. Fourth, merchant diaspora communities and, even more significantly, large groups of transported laborers, whether slave, indentured, or free, have often served as the nuclei for the formation of creole cultures—syncretic amalgamations of two or more cultures with distinctive, creolized languages.

Clearly, therefore, the story of trading tastes—the production of and long-distance exchange in spices, salt, sugar, and silk before 1750—is more than just the tale of evolving industrial and commercial techniques, and certainly much more than premodern macroeconomics in a historical context. It is the story of how trade served as an engine of cultural contact and exchange around the world and helped usher in modern globalization.

Alfred J. Andrea
Professor Emeritus of History
University of Vermont

Acknowledgments

A number of people played crucial roles in making this book happen. Our greatest debt is to Al Andrea for asking us to do the book in the first place and then for being involved with the process at every stage. Indeed, he nearly qualifies for co-author status in addition to his editorial role. Against his better judgment, Charles Cavaliere, our editor on many projects at Prentice Hall, let us embark on this one and lent his full support to it, even though we were supposed to be working on something else. We also wish to thank the photo collection staffs at the Sackler Gallery and the Victoria and Albert Museum for translating our vague and often second-hand descriptions of things seen in their museums into real pictures. The Interlibrary Loan Office at the Dean B. Ellis Library at Arkansas State University (ASU) went beyond the call of duty by tracking down dozens of books and microfilms and then being very liberal about the dates on which they were to be returned. Alex Sydorenko and Pam Hronek supported the project to the extent that ASU's meager budget would permit. Jim Greenwald kindly let us use his personal copy of Pliny's *Natural History*. Bill Maynard provided several useful Silk Road maps. A number of students and colleagues at

Northern Kentucky University helped make this text a reality. Special thanks go to Research Assistant Steve Tully, multi-purpose student Bethany Richter, Department Staff Jan Rachford and Tonya Skelton, Department Chair Jeffrey Williams, and Dean/Provost Gail Wells. Despite the many and manifold contributions of the above parties, they bear no blame for any of the book's shortcomings.

Jonathan also extends thanks to his wonderful wife Ngozi and his wider family for their never-ending patience and support. Erik would like to thank his boys, Oscar and Hans, for being willing to accompany him to Silk Road exhibits and academic conferences and for being quiet while he worked. He also thanks his wife Donna for her support during this project.

About the Authors

Erik Gilbert teaches African history and global history at Arkansas State University. He has done research in Tanzania, Kenya, Yemen, and Oman and is the author of *Dhows and the Colonial Economy of Zanzibar*, 1860–1970 (2004) and co-author (with Jonathan T. Reynolds) of *Africa in World History* (2003).

Jonathan T. Reynolds, A specialist in West Africa, Islam, and global history, has taught at Bayero University, the University of Tennessee, Livingston College (where he received the Aggrey Award for Excellence in Teaching in 1998), and Northern Kentucky University (where he received the Outstanding Junior Faculty Award in 2001). The Fulbright Foundation and the West Africa Research Association have supported his research. With Erik Gilbert, he is the co-author of the highly regarded text, *Africa in World History*.

Introduction

TRADE

The physical texture of our lives is profoundly shaped by trade. Today I am wearing shoes made in Portugal, a sweater made in Sri Lanka, a shirt made in Mauritius, and my pants were made in Mexico. I am drinking coffee that was grown in Central America. My laptop comes from Malaysia. My car, though Japanese, was built in Canada of parts assembled from the four corners of the earth. The same would probably be true of any other American's dining room and driveway.

But there is more to trade than just commodities. Goods rarely travel by themselves. Even in the modern world, where huge ships with tiny crews can haul vast quantities of goods, commodities are culturally "sticky"; people and ideas almost inevitably accompany them. Even if people do not travel in the company of trade goods the way they once did, lots of people seem to have been sucked into the economic and cultural wakes of the imported goods they use. Ideas travel

1

too. At this moment one of my sons is busily sorting Yu Gi Oh cards while his younger brother does likewise with Pokemon cards. Both derive from Japan and represent different facets of the Japanese *anime* tradition. The very Japaneseness of the cards is part of their attraction. American card traders place a special value on cards that are in Japanese even though they cannot read them. So, in this instance trade has given us access not just to Japanese goods but also to Japanese aesthetic ideas, artistic traditions, and, Heaven help us, Hello Kitty. In short, trade not only shapes our tastes in commodities, it shapes other tastes too—culinary, literary, and artistic. It even shapes our worldview and can help shape our religious and spiritual values, as we shall see.

Trade, however, has not always been as extensive as it is now. Not everyone at every time has had access to the broad range of goods that we take for granted. But this is not the first time or place in human history that trade has been a critical part of life. There have been other moments in human history when trade has boomed spectacularly, bringing goods, and the people and ideas that stick to them, to places where they were once rare or unknown. And there has never been a time or place totally devoid of trade. Before there was written history there was trade; indeed, even before there was farming, there was trade. Trade would seem to be a basic human urge.

WHY TRADE?

The obvious answer to the question of why people trade goods is the economic answer. One reason people engage in trade is to get goods that are not available nearby. Archaeologists find that even foragers engaged in trade, sometimes over very long distances to get high quality stone from which to make tools. Certain types of stone, notably the volcanic glass called obsidian, make incredibly sharp tools. But obsidian, which is only found in places where there was once volcanic activity, is uncommon. So it seems to have been traded over long distances—hundreds of miles. In the case of the ancient Aegean Sea there is only one source of obsidian—the island of Melos. But as early as 6500 B.C.E. obsidian shows up on the island of Crete, and by 6000 it is found on the Greek mainland. Although it is clear that boats were involved somehow, the organization of the obsidian trade remains unclear. There might have been specialists who peddled obsidian from place to place. If so, these would have been among the world's first merchants.

More likely is the possibility that these goods were traded from hand to hand and person to person over the distances they moved. This would probably have limited peoples' contact with outsiders and thus the social impact of the trade.

But even in the Stone Age, trade did not solely serve practical needs. In addition to useful things like stone, less obviously useful things were also traded. Seashells often turn up hundreds of miles from the sea. To be sure, shell can be used for toolmaking, but some of these shells apparently served as jewelry. It is easy to imagine how interesting and exotic marine shells might have seemed to people who lived a great distance from the sea. Even if they were not used to make scrappers or other tools, they may have done much to increase the social status of the people who wore them.

This is a critical point. Some trade goods have a social meaning that far exceeds their utility. That your tee shirt was made in Honduras has little social meaning. That your souvenir hat was made in Honduras does have social meaning because it marks you as the sort of person who has been to Honduras. That your Ford Escort was made in Mexico changes nothing; that your Mercedes was made in Germany carries great weight, with its suggestions of sophistication and quality—whether deserved or not. The rarity or exotic nature of trade goods can be a big part of their appeal. Control over trade goods and access to foreign traders can trigger the creation of social hierarchies in egalitarian places and even the creation of states where none existed before.

Some types of trade seem to have no immediate economic purpose at all. In the *kula* trade system of the Trobriand Islands of Melanesia, special armbands and strings of beads are traded from one island to another. Some of the beads circulate in a clockwise pattern and others, which look different, circulate in a counter-clockwise pattern. *Kula* valuables are only exchanged for other *kula* valuables. Thus islanders will get in their boats and make long open water journeys to exchange one type of *kula* valuable for another. The only thing they can do with the valuables they have obtained is to go to another island and exchange them for other *kula* valuables. The result is a steady circulation of goods—goods with no obvious economic utility—in opposite directions in the Trobriand Islands. If these goods have a use, it is clearly social rather than economic. It is the act of exchange (or gift really, because *kula* valuables are often presented to people who have nothing to give in exchange) that is critical, not the beads. People do this precisely because they seek social contacts with outsiders not because they need *kula* valuables. The other reason that the *kula* system exists is that it strengthens the authority and status of chiefs. By organizing the expeditions that travel between the islands, chiefs are able to exhibit their leadership abilities. The *kula* system demonstrates two realities that economists often overlook: people engage in trade for more than strictly economic reasons; and there is a strong relationship between trade and social hierarchy.

This should serve as a caution to us. In our examination of the past we need to be prepared for the possibility that the people whose lives we look at may perceive value in ways that are totally alien to us. Things that to us seem totally outside the realm of the economically valuable— saints' relics or *kula* valuables—may be the focus of trade systems. Clearly value changes over time and place. Somewhere deep in our modern minds is the assumption that people engage in trade and similar activities for reasons that are economically self-serving. And in this we may be wrong. Surely no one, or almost no one, when faced with the choice of having enough to eat or going hungry will choose the latter. However that does not mean that one's next goal will always be the further increase of material wealth. It may instead be religious or social gain rather than material profit. One of the features of human life that the study of trade allows us is to look at the intersection of different systems of value. Trade often brings people with very different views of the world into contact with each other as they make their exchanges.

Much of this book deals less with the economic fallout of trade and more with the social and cultural results of economic exchange. For world historians, one of the main engines of historical change is cross-cultural interaction. They argue that cross-cultural encounter is a major source of human creativity. Encounters between people with totally different ideas about something serve to challenge one's own notions about those beliefs. Trade, along with migration and empire building, is one of the fundamental sources of cross-cultural interactions. So, as we look at trade systems and the movement of goods we also see the spread of ideas, religions, language, technology, and art.

We will also look at the migrations that result from the movement of people that accompanies trade. These movements take two forms. First there are the migrations of merchants. Merchants often move to the places where the goods they buy are produced. In doing so, they create what are called *trade diasporas*. The other type of migration that results from trade is labor migration. In the case of the sugar trade, which will be one of the case studies in this book, the largest forced migration in human history resulted from the labor demands created by the industry that fed Europe's taste for sugar. Whether the voluntary migration of merchant diasporas or the forced migration of the enslaved or the semi-forced migration of the economically disadvantaged in search of work, the social and cultural effects of these movements are every bit as interesting as the economic effects.

MERCHANTS

Merchants occupy a difficult bit of the social landscape. In many traditional societies the merchant's role has been problematic. China's Confucian intelligentsia, for example, placed themselves, the scholar-bureaucrats, at the top of the social hierarchy, peasants in the next slot, artisans in third place, and merchants at the bottom. The justification for this hierarchy was that scholar-bureaucrats provided order, peasants fed everyone, and artisans created essential tools. In contrast, merchants profited by buying goods cheaply and reselling them dearly. This just seemed wrong. They did not seem to be producing anything; in fact it looked as though they were getting rich off the labor of others. Like soldiers, whom the Confucians placed outside of the social order, their presence was a sign that traditional values had been distorted.

Confucian scholars are not unique in their contempt for merchants. As recently as the nineteenth century, to be "in trade" was beneath the dignity of English aristocrats. Circumstances often forced down-at-the-heels aristocrats to marry into merchant families, or to even be silent partners in businesses, but it was never something to be proud of. Even in contemporary North America, surely among the most trade friendly places in history, to be too successful a merchant can cause social opprobrium. Profit is acceptable, profiteering is not. This is doubly true when it comes to the practice of charging interest. Merchants often extend credit to each other and to their customers and charge interest on the credit. Customers the world round like to borrow, but few like to pay for the privilege. Charging high rates of interest (however risky the loan) is a sure way to alienate the public. Banking can be a respected profession, not so for money lending and loan sharking. Many societies place limits on the amount of interest that can be charged, or, as in the case of Islam, forbid it entirely. Thus for merchants to do their work, they often had to come up with

FIGURE I.1   This Italian painting from around 1500 shows a group of Venetian commercial envoys meeting the Mamluk ruler of Syria.

Source: Reunion des Musees Nationaux/Art Resource, NY. Louvre, Paris, France.

subterfuges that allowed them to charge interest without seeming to do so. The most common of these was the rather transparent device of having someone sign a note promising to repay more than the amount that they were actually loaned. While these devices may have met the letter of the law they did little to improve the social standing of merchants in societies where interest was considered immoral.

The wealth of merchants has also made them socially and politically vulnerable. In some places and times wealth has been a magnet for unwanted attention from the state. Monarchs in financial trouble often looked to merchants as a source of quick cash that did not need to be repaid. In some places and times merchants have turned to royal authorities as a source of protection from the depredations of local authorities and have paid for that protection (Figure I.1). In other cases they have been forced just to try to keep their heads down and not appear to be too rich. In some places merchants have developed elaborate traditions of thrift and have carefully avoided ostentatious consumption simply because this helped to avoid unwanted attention. In some societies merchants have been prohibited, by law, from appearing or acting like their social "betters." In other places merchants have forged alliances with those in power and in some instances even used their wealth to pay for their own armies and through them wielded real political power. One of the themes this book will examine is the different social and political role of merchants in the various trade systems we look at. Furthermore, we will look at how the status of merchants has changed over time in these systems.

Merchants are also, in the words of Phillip Curtin, "professional boundary crossers." They often find themselves in places where they are aliens. While movement is part of the human condition and always has been, the average person is distrustful of outsiders, and for much of human history people have placed little trust in people who were not kin or at least very familiar. Merchants who have settled in foreign lands are neither of these and thus often find themselves in an awkward situation. But their ability to function as aliens is a crucial part of their work.

Long-distance trade necessarily involves the interaction of people of very different backgrounds. In addition to the economic role that merchants play in trade, the other crucial role they play is that of "cross-cultural broker," a term also devised by Phillip Curtin. Being a cross-cultural broker involves learning sufficiently well the language and customs of the people with whom one trades so that one can act as an intermediary between two worlds. Even merchants who do not reside with the people with whom they trade need to know enough about their trade partners to earn their trust. Merchants who actually live among their trade partners must have even more developed cultural skills.

By way of example, the Arab merchants who traded on the East African coast were often not permanent residents but stayed there for about half the year. They each had a local patron, who was also a merchant. They stayed in the home of their local patron, who either bought the visiting merchant's goods himself or helped him to find a buyer. The local patron was also responsible for the safety of the visiting merchant and for the safety of his goods and served a guarantor of his honest conduct. As a result, most of the visiting Arabs learned Swahili (the language of the coast) and many also married local women. Often these marriages were to women related to his host, further cementing his relationship to his host.

So important were these relationships that Swahili patricians built their houses with guest apartments and storerooms specifically to accommodate visiting merchants. The regular contact between the

Swahili elite and visiting Arab merchants in turn played a role in spreading Islam and other Arab cultural influence in East Africa. Here, as in many places, the merchants' need to understand local culture for commercial purposes made them ideally suited to the spread and transformation of culture.

Similar examples abound in other places. Indian merchants brought first Hinduism and Buddhism and then Islam to Southeast Asia. Sogdian merchants from the region that today is Uzbekistan brought Zoroastrianism, *then* Buddhism, *then* Manichaeism, *then* Christianity, and *then* Islam to the eastern regions of Central Asia and China. North African merchants brought Islam to West Africa, just as Arab merchants brought Islam to East Africa and to the port cities of western India. Greco-Roman merchants brought their polytheism with them to trade enclaves in India. While their religion never caught on, in fact most of them ultimately became Buddhists, their ideas about how the human form should be represented in art did. Greco-Roman ideas about statues show up in Buddhist art all over Asia. In short, the merchants' historical role extends far beyond the commodities they traded. Their presence as aliens in their host societies seems in the long run to have been just as important.

TRADE AND COMMERCE

Economic historians make a distinction between *trade* and *commerce*. Trade, in this sense, refers to the exchange of high-value, low-bulk goods that can bear easily the cost of transportation over long distances. The best characterization of this type of trade comes from the eighteenth-century Englishman Edward Gibbon, who called the Asian trade of the Roman Empire "a splendid, trifling thing." His point was that the goods that were traded across Asia and the Indian Ocean to Rome were items like silk, spice, gemstones, and drugs. All were gaudy consumer goods used by elites, rather than everyday essentials used by common people. Furthermore they were goods whose size and weight to value ratio very much favored the value side of the equation. One camel load of pearls or silk might of itself be worth a fortune, and thus could justify the cost of making the camel walk a long, long way. By contrast, a camel load of wheat or charcoal would hardly be worth carrying more than a couple of hundred miles, if that. Trade systems like these were found where transport costs were high, usually the case for all long-distance overland trade until the rise of the railroads, and where an elite had the wealth to buy expensive, but ultimately unnecessary things.

That the commodities traded in these systems are unnecessary to normal life is critical. Were the Roman Empire deprived of silk or pearls or the Han Empire deprived of nutmeg and cinnamon, their worlds would not have ended. What would have changed was that some merchants' incomes would have been harmed and some members of the elite would have had one less way of distinguishing themselves from the great unwashed. Trade of this type was often criticized as wasteful. Roman and Chinese social critics often saw this type of trade as a distraction from more sober and economically critical pursuits-producing food, for example.

At the other end of the spectrum is commerce. By commerce, economic historians refer to the exchange of goods of low value and high bulk. By way of example, the trade routes of the Indian Ocean which had been pioneered by sailors and merchants engaged in trade eventually became commercial routes. In 700 most of the long-distance trade on the Indian Ocean would have been in commodities such as spices, silk, ivory, and gold. By 1500 the sea lanes of the Indian Ocean were also being crossed by more and bigger ships carrying timber, cheap cotton cloth, and rice. As ships became more sophisticated and the economic efficiency of ports and distribution systems improved, things like rice could bear the cost of sea transport. As commerce like this became more common, whole cities and regions came to depend on it for the necessities of daily life. K.N. Chaudhuri, one of the leading historians of the Indian Ocean, made the following observation: in 1500 it would be possible for a person in the Persian Gulf to wear cotton cloth from India while eating a bowl of rice also from India while sitting under a roof made of timber imported from East Africa. As he finished the rice he would see a Chinese character—the bowl itself came from China. Unlike the trade systems of earlier periods, the collapse of these commercial systems would be devastating and would harm all society rather than just merchants and elite consumers. Some port cities of the Indian Ocean were utterly dependant on trade. Hormuz, a busy port at the southern end of the Persian Gulf did not even have its own water supply. It relied on ships to bring the water it needed. Aden, which sat at the southern end of the Red Sea, had its own water supply, but was cut off by nearly impenetrable mountains from the farming regions of its hinterland. Its food came to it by sea.

Of course there is no absolute distinction between these two types of exchange. Some commodities start out as trade goods and then become commercial commodities (Figure I.2). Europe's pepper trade was once "a splendid, trifling thing." Pepper from India came up the Red Sea to Egypt where it was sold to Venetian merchants who resided in the Egyptian port city of Alexandria. The Venetians then sent an annual convoy from Alexandria to Antwerp, where they were able to charge such high prices that pepper was a luxury good. This was doubly the case for the fine spices—cloves, nutmeg, mace, and cinnamon. These were so rare and expensive that they were used in banquet foods and as a form of ostentation.

But things change. Around 1500 the Portuguese opened a sea route to India and broke the Venetian monopoly on pepper. In the following century pepper went from being a luxury good to being fairly commonplace. By the seventeenth century it was common for European sailors—as far from members of the elite as one could find—to carry with them little bags of pepper. By the eighteenth century the fine spices were cheap enough that they were used to flavor wines and ales.

The other factor to bear in mind is that both types of exchange can co-exist. Arab and Indian merchants came to East Africa to buy gold. But a shipload of gold is probably more gold than any one merchant or even consortium of merchants could afford. And even if they could afford it they probably would not want to risk that much gold in a single ship. So sea captains coming to East Africa bought relatively small quantities of gold and then had to decide what to do with the rest of the space in their holds. Ships need to carry a certain amount of weight so that they will be stable. One option was to buy something bulky that could be resold at home. One such ballast cargo was mangrove wood, which is abundant and cheap in East Africa. Had the same captain carried only mangrove wood, he might have made so tiny a profit that the voyage would not have been worth it. Profit from the gold was the main reason for the voyage, but profit from the timber was a nice addition. Thus trade in gold stimulated commerce in timber.

Indeed whole economies have been shaped by the need for ballast to accompany high-value cargoes. Cowry shells (the shells of an ocean mollusk) were once used in much of South Asia and parts of Africa as a so-called "humble currency." One theory about how cowries came to be used this way is that ships going to the Maldive islands (home to the shells) carrying high value cargoes of cloth needed ballast for the

FIGURE I.2 These low structures were both home and shop to their merchant owners.

Source: Bibliotheque Nationale de France.

voyage back to India. Cowries, which had a sort of aesthetic appeal, were used and eventually came to be used as a currency.

Periodization

The year 1750 is generally considered a pivotal date in world history, which is why it marks the end of the period that this book set out to examine. This year is considered the dividing line between the early modern period and the modern period. Although these terms were originally derived from European history, most world historians accept that they have broader application. After 1750, the world, not just Europe, was on the path to modernity. So the world this book has examined is considered "pre-modern."

Trade Systems

This book is organized around the production and exchange of four particular commodities: spice, salt, sugar, and silk. Although each of these commodities has been traded over huge areas, each is also associated with a particular geographical area and a particular cultural and economic system.

Spices were central to the Indian Ocean trading world and it was the lure of pepper and the fine spices that originally brought Europeans to the Indian Ocean. Ultimately the trade networks that moved spice would carry it well beyond the confines of the Indian Ocean, but our study of the spice trade will focus on the warm waters of the Indian Ocean.

Salt is, of course, consumed nearly universally. Indeed, for people who live primarily on plant foods it is essential to life. Salt features in the trade of Europe, where mines in Poland supplied the Baltic herring fishery with salt to preserve fish. Salt was also part of the trade of the western Indian Ocean—vessels traveling to East Africa from the Persian Gulf would carry salt to exchange for mangrove wood. Salt was traded and taxed just about everywhere, but it is especially associated with the trade system that stretched across the Sahara from North Africa to the trade-oriented cities of West African *Sahel*, or grasslands just south of the Sahara. There salt was not just a feature of a broader trade system, it was, along with gold, the central commodity, the *raison d'etre* for the whole system.

As was the case with spice, sugar was also associated with an ocean—this time the Atlantic. The story of sugar, despite sugar's popularity in the Middle East and India, and its ancient roots in New Guinea, is ultimately about the creation of the Atlantic plantation system. Sugar was the central commodity in an economic system that moved slaves from Africa and indentured servants from Europe to produce sugar in the Americas for consumption throughout Europe.

Whereas sugar fed all classes, silk was (and still is) a favorite of elites throughout the Old World. In the fifteenth century West Africans imported silk cloth, unraveled it and rewove it with cotton thread to make what is called silk-shot cloth. East African elites likewise had a taste for silk , as did their counterparts in South and Southeast Asia. Despite this near universal taste for silk as a status symbol, the fabric is especially associated with the so-called Silk Road. This complex network of caravan routes stretched from China to the Mediterranean Sea, and, despite some downturns, it remained commercially vibrant from the second century B.C.E. into the fifteenth century C.E. Though silk was not the only commodity that moved along these caravan routes it was the glamor commodity of the trade system.

WHY SPICE?

As is true of some of the other commodities in this study, spices have gone from expensive luxury goods to relatively commonplace consumer goods. Probably even the most ill-equipped kitchen has at least a bit of black pepper in it and maybe some cinnamon. More enthusiastic cooks are likely to have nutmeg, cloves, vanilla, mace, and allspice in the spice rack. Although these spices—pepper not included—have come down in value over the centuries, they are still moderately expensive. What has changed is their relative price and their cultural and economic significance. Spice was once so valuable that it created balance of payment problems for the Roman Empire. Control over the spice trade made the Italian city-state of Venice wealthy and contributed to the wealth of Fatimid Egypt (969–1171). For European noblemen, the consumption of spice was one way of showing off their wealth. In South and Southeast Asia, spices were more common and less of a luxury, but still their production and distribution was a major focus of regional economies. Spices were once at the center of geopolitical considerations, with various powers vying for control of spice islands, using brutal intimidation to maintain control of their monopolies over the production of certain spices, and trying to find cheap substitutes for the real spices. *As such, the spice trade is a perfect example of the transition from trade to commerce.* In the first century C.E. pepper was a high-value trade item sought after by status-conscious Romans and Chinese. By 1750 pepper was used to fill empty cargo spaces in ships, little more than ballast with a market price. The reason for the drop in price has everything to do with changes in the way pepper and other spices were transported and distributed and very little to do with how they were produced. Most spices do not lend themselves to mechanized agriculture and are produced today in much the same way they were a thousand years ago.

The story of the spice is also the story of a revolution in transportation and in the business methods of merchants.

The same transportation revolution that was responsible for the dramatic drop in the price and hence the social meaning of spice made the spice trade a vehicle for a great deal of cross-cultural interaction. The Roman desire for pepper brought merchants from the empire to the ports of western India, some of whom became permanent residents and even converted to Buddhism. Others returned to the Mediterranean contributing to a boom in Roman knowledge of the Indian Ocean. The spice trade also brought Indian merchants to Southeast Asia, which contributed to the Indianization of court life and religion in Southeast Asia. Chinese merchants also came to Southeast Asia giving some areas of the region a distinctly Chinese flavor. Later as Europeans arrived in significant numbers after 1500, the creation of empires, which were devoted in part to controlling the spice trade, resulted in Europe's first full encounter with South and East Asia, which had profound consequences for Asia, Europe, and even Africa.

The geographical center of the spice trade was the Indian Ocean. All of the major spices were grown in the lands of the Indian Ocean, either in the southern parts of the Indian subcontinent or in the islands of what is now Indonesia. Thus, all the great spice ports, all the mercantile adventures, all the empire building, and the other dramas of the spice trade took place in the Indian Ocean. So in looking at the history of the spice trade we will also be looking at the history of the Indian Ocean region. This is important because it was the first ocean (as opposed to the Mediterranean Sea) to serve as the focus of a commercial system. Long before there was an Atlantic system (the subject of the sugar chapter) or a "Pacific century," there was a busy commercial and cultural world centered on the Indian Ocean. To be sure, spice was not the only commodity that was exchanged within the Indian Ocean commercial system. Cloth, timber, foodstuffs, and ceramics were also important, but spice played a crucial role. To a greater extent than any of the other commodities that moved on the Indian Ocean, spice could bear the cost of transportation beyond the confines of the ocean. Thus, unlike timber or rice, spice was brought by sea from India to the head of the Red Sea or the Persian Gulf, transported overland to the Mediterranean, and then by sea again to Italy or even to the Low Countries for distribution throughout Europe. Spice, then, was a crucial point of connection between the Indian Ocean and the Mediterranean, and to a lesser extent to the South China Sea. As a result, what

Europeans knew about the Indian Ocean was shaped by their knowledge of the spice trade, and when Europeans sought entrée into the commercial world of the Indian Ocean, it was spice they were after. When Christopher Columbus set out across the Atlantic, one of his goals was to get access to the spice markets of the Indian Ocean. When Vasco da Gama set out for India by sailing around Africa, it was pepper he was looking for. When the Portuguese set up their imperial outpost in Goa, part of the calculation was the city's proximity to the pepper ports of southern India.

Not just Europeans were interested in Indian Ocean spices. The Chinese consumed huge quantities of pepper, as well as other spices. When the Ming Empire sent its representatives into the Indian Ocean in the fifteenth century, their ships visited the Southeast Asian port of Malacca (a major trans-shipment point for cloves and nutmeg) and Calicut, the same south Indian pepper port that da Gama would visit 80 years later.

In short, spices are about as historically significant as a commodity can get. From very early times they have been traded across long distances, bringing together people as disparate as Europeans and Southeast Asians, sometimes only as the far ends of a long commodity chain and sometimes face to face. Spices have served as signs of social status, and as currency. They have encouraged merchant diasporas. They have triggered voyages of discovery and motivated empire builders.

WHY SALT?

Perhaps few commodities reflect the transformation in notions of value brought about by globalization and industrialization as well as does salt. Nowadays, salt seems to be everywhere. Anybody who wants it can get it. A handful of pure, processed, sodium chloride can be had just about anywhere in the world for a very small amount of money. Restaurants offer shakers of it for free on the table, and one can get packets of it "to go" by the handful just by asking. Cities in northerly climes stockpile mountains of it to dump on roads to melt snow and ice. In fact, the prevalence of salt in our lives seems more a bane than a boon. We might like the way it tastes, but too much salt in our food leads to health problems, such as hypertension. Salt on the roads makes our cars rust.

But, the contemporary ubiquity and uniformity of salt is a rather new development in terms of world history. Prior to the nineteenth century, salt was rare and valuable to the degree that it made perfect sense to fight over it. Indeed, the historian Paul Lovejoy has argued that prior to a couple of hundred years ago, salt played much the same critical role in economies (and politics) that oil does today. Through production or trade, salt was often the key source of revenue for states. Indeed, rather than being seen as injurious to health, salt was seen as essential to life. And it is. Our bodies cannot process liquids or carry out various metabolic processes without a certain amount of salt. On average, an individual needs about 4.5 kilograms of salt a year, and the quantity goes up in hotter climes, where individuals lose salt through extensive sweating. Getting enough salt was a particular problem for societies that practiced sedentary agriculture. Staple grain crops such as wheat, rice, maize, or millet produced remarkable food surpluses that allowed societies to create complex relationships between farmers, craftspeople, merchants, and rulers, but they also created a potentially unhealthy diet low in salt. Foraging and pastoralist peoples usually were able to get plenty of salt from their varied diets and fairly regular intake of meat, but diets made up primarily of grains and vegetables lack enough salt to ensure proper biological processes. Further, salt was critical not only in terms of diet, but was also useful in many other ways. The curing of meat and fish, the pickling of vegetables, and the making of cheese (all salt-intensive processes) are methods used by various human societies to store food over long periods. Salt was not only a necessary part of people's diets, but it was also a way people insured that they would have food between growing seasons or when crops failed for one reason or another. Salt was a matter of health and a key element in food security.

Salt, however, was not only critical in terms of diet and food storage. As a chemical, salt is also important to a number of industrial practices. It also played a critical role in early medicine. Central to our understanding of the multiple roles played by early salt is the fact that one should speak of "salts" rather than salt. Modern table salt is a highly refined product—almost completely pure sodium chloride (often with iodine added to help prevent goiter). In many pre-modern human societies, however, there was a large variety of salts to choose from. Different recipes might call for different varieties of salt, varying not only in source and means of production but also in terms of chemical composition. Some varieties of salt could have potent biological effects, and were thus used as medicines. Others were outright poisonous, but had valuable industrial applications in such processes as curing leather or smelting metals. The differences in chemical composition of available salts reflected the environmental and geological conditions of different settings, and often had substantial impact on local tastes in salt and, as we shall see, salt production and trade. Local societies had to learn to extract salt from the resources available, or make arrangements to import it from afar.

Only a few people in the pre-modern world, such as those residing near the Dead Sea region of Israel, were blessed with easily available sources of high-quality salt. Most others had to go to great lengths to find or produce salt. The dried lakebeds of former lakes and seas, such as are found in the Western Sahara in Africa or Mojave in North America, are often excellent sources of salt. Similarly, the shores of existing lakes in arid regions can yield a great variety of salts during the dry season when waters recede. Unfortunately, the inhospitable nature of desert environments, as we shall see, made access to and transport of this valuable commodity difficult. Underground salt domes are a fairly common geological feature, but prior to the development of modern drilling techniques they were hard to find and the salt was hard to extract. There is a reason we use the phrase "back to the salt mines" to refer to unpleasant work. Seawater, obviously, was also a source, but the relatively low concentration of salt in seawater made the process laborious and fuel-intensive. Just boiling seawater does not yield a lot of, or very high-quality, salt. Societies in coastal regions thus learned to concentrate the brine via various techniques before boiling it. Natural brine springs can also be a source of highly concentrated salt water. The point here is that getting salt was not easy. In some locales, getting salt meant traveling long distances in harsh environments. In others, salt production meant the development of sophisticated techniques to concentrate brine and then remove the salt—often requiring a number of complex steps and considerable levels of supporting container and fuel technology. *Salt production, in many ways, was the world's first industry.*

Because salt was both rare and difficult to produce, it often was transported long distances to meet demand. Further, salt was high value. High-quality salt could be traded as a luxury, and even less refined varieties of salt were still high in value. A small amount could represent a considerable store of wealth. It was not unheard to trade salt for rare spices or other high-value items. While rumors of salt being exchanged on par with gold are probably just that, a big pile of salt could certainly get a nice, if somewhat smaller, pile of gold in return. Salt was thus a critical component in early long-distance trade networks. In many locales, salt even became the mode of exchange—money itself.

In fact, our modern term "salary" owes its origin to the Latin *salarium*, or the "salt allowance" paid to Roman soldiers (either in salt or to buy salt).

Finally, wherever there are scarce and valuable commodities, there is usually a government interested in controlling them. Many governments found in salt production and trade an almost irresistible way to extract wealth from their subject populations either through the control of production and distribution or via control and taxation of trade across their borders. Because salt was not only rare but also essential to life, it was the perfect means by which states could extract or produce the wealth to pay for infrastructure, armies, or impressive looking palaces. As such, salt was critical to government revenue and power.

Taken as a whole, all these factors mean that salt touched on almost every aspect of the lives of most pre-modern farming societies. The availability and variety of salt could determine the types of food people ate. Efforts to produce salt could encourage technological innovation and influence the nature and allocation of labor. Trade linkages that brought salt could also lead to substantial cultural exchange between societies. And, finally, salt could play a critical role in determining the very nature of the relationship between the rulers and the ruled. Such is the nature of commodity and culture.

WHY SUGAR?

Refined sugar is so ubiquitous today that it is impossible to avoid completely. It is in our soft drinks, our snacks, and most processed foods. Even fundamentally savory foods, such as commercial tomato sauce, are full of sweeteners. There is sugar in ketchup, in bread, in breakfast cereal, and in salsa. Sugar is a central part of the modern diet and forms a significant portion of the total calories consumed throughout the world, and because sugar is cheap, the poor eat disproportionately large amounts of it.

This is a relatively new phenomenon. Until the eighteenth century, sugar, especially in its white, or refined, form, was a luxury food. Indeed, if we go back to before the year 1000, sugar was virtually unknown in Europe. The Venerable Bede, an English monk of the eighth century, left at his death a small quantity of spice, which included a few ounces of sugar, but other than that there is next to nothing written about sugar in Western Europe until after 1000. During the fifteenth and sixteenth centuries, however, Europe's recently colonized

Atlantic islands of Madeira and the Canaries were busy producing sugar to meet the growing European demand for this sweetener.

By the end of the sixteenth century, the Portuguese were growing sugar in Brazil, and a century later the English, Dutch, and French were doing likewise in the islands of the Caribbean. By the nineteenth century, sugar production for European consumption had moved out of the Atlantic and into the Indian Ocean and even the Pacific. The spread of plantation-style sugar production throughout the tropics by itself would make the sugar trade an interesting topic to world historians. For our purposes, the trade in sugar is also interesting because it is a perfect example of a trade good becoming a commercial commodity. What was once a rare and precious substance in Europe later became so cheap that it was a crucial part of the English working-class diet in the nineteenth century.

But there is more. Sugar production has almost always been done by laborers working under some degree of compulsion. Often sugar plantation workers were slaves. Sometimes they were indentured servants or were bound by contracts that effectively made them temporary slaves. What this meant was that the sugar trade was closely linked to the slave trade or later to trade in contract workers. As recently as the early twentieth century, so-called Blackbirders transported forcibly indentured, often kidnapped, "contract" workers from New Guinea and elsewhere to work on the sugar plantations of northern Australia. The labor demands of sugar plantations were the primary force behind the Atlantic slave trade, but sugar also drew South Asians to Trinidad in the Caribbean, Suriname in South America, and Fiji in the Pacific. It took Africans and South Asians to the sugar islands of the Indian Ocean, creating complex creole societies, in which disparate cultures, languages, and gene pools fused to create new, hybrid entities. *Thus, the story of sugar is also the story of the biggest movements of coerced labor in the history of the pre-modern world, but that story also includes the creation of syncretic cultures and languages.*

Another crucial aspect of the sugar trade is that processed sugar was among the first consumer goods to be widely used by people who lived far from its place of production. Sugar cane can only grow in tropical or sub-tropical places, and it prefers the former. Thus, until the nineteenth-century discovery of a process for extracting sugar from sugar beets, all of the sugar consumed by northern Europeans came from elsewhere—often a very distant elsewhere. However, unlike some other luxury goods that traveled long distances, pepper, for example, this was one where production and transportation were organized by Europeans.

The pepper that Europeans ate was purchased from South Asians. The sugar that Europeans ate was produced on plantations owned by Europeans in colonies claimed by Europeans states. The spice trade motivated the imperial ambitions of Europeans in Asia insofar as they established trading enclaves in distant lands in and around the Indian Ocean, but sugar led to a different types of imperial structures in the Americas based on exploited labor managed by European settlers.

The final reason the sugar trade is so interesting is found in the economic organization of sugar plantations. Because of the unique demands of sugar production, sugar plantations are part farm and part factory. They combine elements of an older agricultural world with elements of the emerging industrial world. Early plantation owners may have tried to mimic the lifestyles of European landed aristocrats, but they organized, supervised, and disciplined their workers in ways much more like that of the industrial capitalist world that would emerge in the nineteenth century. It would be difficult to argue that Europe's industrial revolution was born out of the sugar trade—though the argument has been made, but it is clear that the sugar industry foreshadowed some elements of the industrial revolution.

The sugar trade created an astonishing web of connections. It brought enslaved Africans, Europeans (both free and indentured), and South Asians to the New World. It put exotic tropical food on the tables of Europeans. And over time the importance of sugar in the European diet grew to the point that by the end of the nineteenth century fully 20 percent of the calories consumed by the English working class came from sugar. Thus the lives of Europeans, Africans, and Americans were all brought together—for better and worse—by sugar. Unlike other long-distance trade, where merchants were the main agents of cross-cultural interaction, in the sugar trade it was the people involved in production who played that role. As a result, the focus of this chapter is different from other chapters in the book. Here merchants will be in the background, and the slaves and indentured servants who worked on sugar plantation often thousands of miles from their homes will be in the foreground.

WHY SILK?

If the spice trade is largely the story of the Indian Ocean, then silk's history is bound up in the caravan towns of Central Asia and the Buddhist monasteries of western China, which dotted the fabled Silk Road. The

Silk Road was not a single road but rather a complex and shifting system of overland trade routes that linked China to the markets of Central Asia, India, the Middle East, and the Mediterranean from the second century B.C.E. to about 1500 C.E. These trade routes carried many other commodities, most notably jade, glass, coral, drugs, spices, ceramicware, lacquerware, and cotton, but none had the depth of social meaning that silk did. The use of the term "Silk Road" is a modern convention. It was coined by the Baron Ferdinand von Richtofen in 1877, though he used the more accurate, but less mellifluous plural form "Seidenstrassen" or Silk Roads. (If the name seems familiar, it is because he was the uncle of another Baron von Richtofen, the World War I fighter ace and Snoopy's nemesis.) No one knows which of the many commodities that moved along these trade routes was the most economically important, and it seems quite likely that silk was overshadowed economically by more mundane trade goods. Furthermore, silk also left China by sea, especially at times of political instability in Central Asia. So although Richtofen's term may not have been perfectly accurate in economic terms, it makes a certain amount of sense in cultural terms. Of the many things China produced, few have been as desired by outsiders as silk.

For the past one hundred years, the Silk Road has captured the imagination of both Asians and Europeans. Most of the overland trade routes across Asia fell into decline in the sixteenth and seventeenth centuries as ships and oceanic trading routes became evermore efficient. In the centuries that followed, both Asians and Europeans more or less forgot that there was a time when Chinese empires had reached out across Eurasia seeking horses and other exotic occidental trade goods, and likewise that the people of what the Chinese termed the "western lands" (a generic term that covered people as diverse as Persians, Indians, and Romans) were equally eager to obtain China's exotica, especially its silk cloth. Interest in the history of these ancient trade routes revived in the late nineteenth and early twentieth centuries with the discovery, mostly by western adventurer-scholars, of huge troves of Buddhist art and literature (as well as the art and sacred texts of other religions, including Christianity) in the ruined oasis towns and Buddhist shrines of western China. Many of these men operated on the fine line between legitimate archeology and reckless plundering. One of them, the American Langdon Warner, might have served as a model for the Indiana Jones movie character. Eventually, the Chinese government, alarmed by the removal of so much of their cultural heritage, clamped down on this activity. Interest in the Silk Road continued more or less unabated as Chinese scholars took over excavation and study of the oasis towns and other Silk Road sites.

Excavations at Silk Road sites and study of the artifacts and texts found there show beyond any doubt that the Silk Road was one of the great conduits for cross-cultural interaction in Eurasia. One Chinese scholar has compared the opening of the Silk Road and China's subsequent encounter with the "Western Lands" with Columbus' opening of a sea route to the Americas. The merchants, missionaries, pilgrims, diplomats, and armies that traveled along the Silk Road's many routes were vehicles for the transmission of artistic styles, fashions in dance, music, and costume, flora and fauna of every sort, technological innovations, games and sports, and, perhaps most important, religions. Buddhism, Zoroastrianism, Manichaeism, Christianity, and Islam, and even Judaism, traveled far from their homelands to points along the Silk Road and to China itself. And from China many of these cultural treasures from the Silk Road, especially Buddhism, moved into Korea and Japan. Moreover, the religions and other ideas and expressions that were shared and exchanged in caravan stops in Central Asia often took on new forms as they were shaped by the cultures of their new hosts. In a time when encounters between civilizations are termed "clashes" and assumed by some to be a zero-sum winner-take-all struggle, the story of the Silk Road reminds us that cross-cultural encounter also can enrich those who are open to foreign ideas.

CONNECTED COMMODITIES

Before plunging into the case studies, we would like to leave you with a few observations. We have organized this book around four commodities and their associated trade systems. This is a way of modeling the past, and as such has its virtues and failings. Its biggest virtue is that it provides a relatively simple means of looking at complex commercial networks. Its biggest failing is that it falsely suggests that these businesses were somehow discrete economic systems. As you will see when you get to the documents, the real world is a much messier place than our division suggests. Silk merchants also dealt in spices. The sugar trade was closely tied to textiles, slaves, and, on some levels, the spice trade. Spice merchants also bought and sold silk, along with pots and pans, drugs, gems, gold, cotton, and scented woods.

CHAPTER

1

The Spice Trade

THE SPICE PARADOX

Perhaps the most puzzling thing about spices is that they are so unessential. All of the other commodities examined in detail in this book have more practical use. Salt is an essential part of our diet. Silk may not be essential, but it is a practical and comfortable way of clothing a body. Likewise, sugar is not necessary, but it is a good fuel for the mammalian body. In fact, sugar produces more calories per acre than another crop. Probably all of us can imagine leading full and meaningful lives without cloves, nutmeg, or cinnamon. Not having pepper might mean bland food, but the other spices are hard to imagine at the center of global geopolitics. But they once were. So perhaps the best place to begin an exploration of the spice trade is not with production or distribution, but with consumption.

Pepper

Pepper has three forms, black, long, and white, and all originated in India. Long pepper grows in northern India and is harvested before it ripens. The seeds are dried and yield a pepper that is generally considered inferior to black pepper. It is called "long" because the seeds stay together in an oblong cluster or pod. In late medieval Europe long pepper was widely consumed, but it is rarely seen today in the West. However, it remains popular in India, where its distinctive taste is preferred in some dishes.

Black pepper, the standard form of pepper known throughout the world today, is grown in the hotter and wetter reaches of southern India. The berries are harvested when red and then left to ferment, during which time a fungus causes the skins to wither and blacken. White pepper comes from the same plant, but instead of allowing the fermentation process to take place, the skins are rubbed off leaving just the white inner seed. White pepper tastes much the same as black pepper but is a bit milder. It also has the virtue of not putting black flecks into white sauces, once a serious *faux pas*. Red and green forms of black pepper are obtained by harvesting the seeds while they are still green, or by allowing them to ripen to red and skipping the fermentation step. Red and green forms of black pepper have only recently come in to fashion.

Malagueta pepper, which is botanically different from Indian pepper but tastes similar, grows in West Africa and has been used as a much cheaper substitute. It is also worth noting that capsicum, or American chili peppers, are not related to old world peppers. Interestingly though, chilies became widely popular in the spice growing areas of Asia upon being introduced by the Portuguese. Some of the world's hottest and most capsicum-filled foods are eaten in South India and Southeast Asia, both major producers of spices.

Before and after 1500, Indian pepper was used for a variety of purposes. First and foremost is its use for flavoring savory dishes. Black pepper is a component of many of the spice combinations that go into the Indian *garam masala*, a powder made by roasting and grinding various spices and used to flavor everything from salads to curries. Some of the spice combinations used in the Arab world to flavor grilled meats and to make condiments also use black pepper (Figure 1.1).

The Romans used pepper in large quantities. Medieval Europeans also were fond of it, in part because its pungent flavor helped to mask

FIGURE 1.1   "Empress" pepper pot. This is a *piperatorium* (pepper pot), from a hoard of valuables buried in the fifth century C.E. in Roman Britain. Pepper was valuable enough that the items used to store and display it were treasures worth burying along with the jewelry and coins that make up the rest of the hoard. It is made of silver and depicts a generic empress.

Source: © The British Museum.

the taste of the salt-cured meats they ate. It is basically untrue, as one sometimes hears, that Europeans need Asian spices to cover the taste of the "rotten meat" they ate. The whole point of curing meat in salt was to prevent its spoiling. Medieval Europeans also used locally available flavorings, such as honey, onions, garlic, and various herbs, to make cured meats taste better. It is also worth pointing out that for the vast majority of medieval Europeans, flavoring meat was not an urgent problem. Meat eating and the use of spice was confined to relatively small number of wealthy people. By the seventeenth century the use of pepper in Europe was more widespread. Not only could common people afford it, but it started to turn up in beverages, such as beers and wine. It was also added to fruit and sweets occasionally.

Cloves

Cloves originate from the buds of a tree that is native to a few islands in Indonesia. Picked before the flowers can open and then dried, the resulting spices look like little nails, and our word for them derives from the Latin *clavus*, which means "nail." They have a strong, aromatic taste, which makes them popular with Asian and Arab cooks. For example, they are an essential ingredient in the classic Chinese five spice mixture and in many north Indian *garam masalas*. In the modern West, cloves are far less popular and are mostly used in baked sweets, such as spice cake. In Roman and medieval Europe, cloves were used to flavor meats much more extensively than we do now. One relic of this tradition is the studding of hams with cloves, but it was once common to eat beef and pork dishes with liberal amount of cloves in the sauce—at least for those who could afford the extravagance. Cloves, like many of the fine spices, were also considered an aid to the digestion. For those who could afford not just to indulge in meat, but to over indulge, cloves not only made the meat tasty, they helped the gourmand digest it.

Cloves have other interesting qualities. Clove oil is a natural anesthetic. Before modern dentistry, clove oil was used to soothe toothaches. Chew a clove, and you will notice a slight numbing effect on your tongue and gums. Cloves were also desired as a breath freshener. As early as the Han period in China, people wishing to appear before the emperor were expected to chew cloves so that their breath would not offend. Many mouth washes still contain eugenol, which is the main component of clove oil. More recently Indonesians have begun to smoke cloves, usually mixed with tobacco. Currently Indonesia is the world's largest consumer of cloves, mostly for use in clove cigarettes. Curiously, Indonesians make very little culinary use of cloves.

Nutmeg

Nutmeg is indigenous to roughly the same area of Indonesia that is home to the clove tree. Also like cloves, nutmeg is a tree crop. The part of the nutmeg that is eaten is not actually a nut—it is more like the stone of an apricot. Mace, which is also a spice, is the leathery substance that surrounds the nutmeg. It is usually sold separately in the US, but sometimes one finds a nutmeg sold with the mace intact. Nutmeg has a more delicate and subtle flavor than cloves, and mace is, if anything, less assertive. The flavor of nutmeg will probably be known best to Americans from eggnog, in which nutmeg is the dominant spice.

Nutmeg is widely used to flavor meat dishes in Northern India and much of the Middle East. It is part of the classic French spice combination *quatre epices* which contains white pepper, nutmeg, cloves, and ginger. *Quatre epices* is used to flavor stewed meats and as such harkens back to a time when Europeans regularly used fine spices in the preparation of meat dishes. When nutmeg was first introduced to Europe, by the Arabs, it was used to flavor beer.

Like cloves, nutmegs also have non-culinary uses. Some of the alkaloids in nutmeg are psychoactive. Consumed in large quantities, nutmegs produce a cheap but viciously nasty high. Do not try this at home though; the amount of nutmeg needed to produce the desired effect is more than enough to cause horrible nausea. One nutmeg abuser reports that he was unable to tolerate the smell of nutmeg for almost a decade after his pursuit of a cheap, but spicy, high.

Cinnamon

Two different spices are called by the name cinnamon: cassia, which is native to China, and Ceylon cinnamon, which is native to Sri Lanka (formerly called Ceylon). Both are made from the bark of related but different trees. They have similar tastes, though in the West, at least, the flavor of Ceylon cinnamon is considered superior.

Cinnamon is a critical ingredient in many south Asian dishes, and it was used in medieval Europe to prepare meats, often in combination with the other fine spices. It has since lost favor among most Western cooks (except the Greeks) and has, like the other fine spices, been relegated mostly to the preparation of sweets. Like the other fine spices, it was once used to flavor wine, a use that continues in mulled wine. The Ethiopian spice mixture *berebere* typically contains cinnamon. Cinnamon has also caught the attention of New World cooks and has become a standard ingredient in some Mexican moles.

THE FIRST GLOBAL FOODS

Spices were probably the first global foods. Long before other food-stuffs could bear the cost of long-distance transportation, people all over the Afro-Eurasian World, and after 1500 in the Americas, as well, were able to share a taste for certain flavors. While a European meal in 1450 might feature bread, meat, and grape wine, a north Indian meal might consist of lentils, rice and chapattis, and a Chinese meal might center on rice, rice wine, and meat. All of these would probably have been grown or raised quite near to the place where they were consumed. But each of these meals would have been seasoned with spices that were imported from the same places. The merchants who bought, sold, and transported these spices over long distances were truly trading in tastes.

THE SPICE TRADE IN CLASSICAL TIMES

By the end of the first century B.C.E., China's Han empire and the Roman Empire were equally prosperous, stable, and economically dynamic, and each had a wealthy elite with a growing interest in lux-ury housing, clothing, and food. The anthropologist Jack Goody has argued in *Food and Love* that the notion of romantic love and high cui-sine are exclusively found in socially stratified societies. As far as high cuisine is concerned, his argument is that in more egalitarian societies everyone eats pretty much the same thing. There may be special foods for special occasions, but in general everyone eats the same basic food, and they do so mostly to stay alive. In contrast, societies that generate a significant economic surplus and have an elite with disproportionate access to that surplus have the time to invent more interesting foods for pleasure and as a form of social expression. To eat rare and unusual foods, especially foods from far away, is a way of indicating one's high social status. Spices, especially the fine spices, are thus a perfect form of conspicuous consumption.

Occasional references to spice in the Hebrew Bible and in Greek texts suggest that small quantities of spices were available in the pre-Roman Mediterranean. But the Han-Roman period caused a major expansion of the trade for two reasons: the rise of a large class of potential consumers of luxury goods; and Han China's deep penetration into Central Asia. Han military outposts reached as far west as Afghanistan, providing critical security for overland trade. The rise of the Parthian and Kushan empires, respectively in Persia and Iraq and parts of Central Asia and northern India, further increased the security of Eurasian trade routes.

Sea lanes also became safer, especially in the Indian Ocean. By the first century C.E. the Roman navy was patrolling the Red Sea in order to suppress piracy, and Greco-Roman merchants ventured into the Indian Ocean, following trade routes already established by Arab, Indian and Persian merchants.

These trade routes were made possible by the monsoon winds. There are two monsoons. The northeast monsoon, which blows from late November to April out of the northeast, is a hot, dry, steady wind much loved by sailors, because the sea is relatively calm, the wind dependable, and storms are rare. By contrast, the southwest monsoon, which blows from late April to September, is more troublesome to sailors. Carrying moisture off the sea to much of southern Asia, it is accompanied often by violent winds and rough seas. Nonetheless, by the time of the Han-Roman period sailors had learned to make good use of both monsoons which allowed Indian Ocean sailors to have tail-winds going out and returning, depending on the time of the year. The same wind reversal patterns worked for voyages between India and the Persian Gulf, India and East Africa, India and Southeast Asia, and China and Southeast Asia. The result was a system of oceanic trade not found on any other ocean except the much smaller Mediterranean. Unlike the Mediterranean, however, which links ecologically similar regions, the waters of the Indian Ocean touched places as different as the tropical islands of Southeast Asia, home to the nutmeg and clove tree, the cotton growing regions of Gujarat, the pepper-producing areas of southern India, and the desiccated incense-producing regions of the southern Arabian Peninsula.

The other effect of the monsoons was a segmentation of the commercial system. Because one could not easily make the voyage from

Arabia to Southeast Asia or China in a single monsoon season, sailors developed circuits that they could make in a single year. Arabs, and a few Greco-Romans, controlled the routes between the Arabian Peninsula and East Africa. Arabs and Indians made the voyages between India and the Persian Gulf. Indians controlled the routes between South India and Southeast Asia, and the Chinese controlled the routes between Southeast Asia and China. These routes were not controlled by military force; rather, it was habit, proximity, and knowledge that allowed one group or another to dominate a particular trade route. The result of this segmentation was regional zones of cross-cultural interaction that lasted long after the collapse of the Han and Roman Empires.

It is hard to judge the economic scale and importance of the spice trade during this period. Clearly in spice-producing areas participation in the trade was central to the local economy. What is harder to judge is the extent to which these trades affected the broader economies of China, Rome, and India. The Roman encyclopedist Pliny the Elder, estimated in the first century that Rome annually expended 12,500,000 *denarii* (small silver coins) in its trade with India. A further 12,500,000 was spent on the trade with Arabia, and China. To put this in perspective, an average daily wage was 1 to 2 denarii, and the Emperor Tiberius' treasury amounted to 750,000 denarii. Three centuries later when Rome was in decline, Alaric, a Goth who had besieged Rome, was given three thousand pounds of pepper from an imperial stockpile as a ransom for the city. Rome taxed the fine spices at rates as high as 25 percent, but pepper was not taxed, suggesting that it was considered more of a necessity than a luxury. In short the scale and economic importance of the trade seems to have been greater than the non-essential nature of the products would suggest. But what of the cultural fallout from the trade? How did the movement of merchants and their goods reshape the cultural landscape of the lands around the Indian Ocean?

THE SPICE TRADE AND CROSS-CULTURAL INTERACTION IN THE CLASSICAL PERIOD

Cross-cultural encounters at this time were numerous and extensive, but let us focus on two areas of particular interest: Rome's encounter with India and the Indian encounter with Southeast Asia.

Romans in India

During the first several centuries C.E., Romans constructed trade posts in India, where some converted to Buddhism, and a few Romans seem to have traveled as far afield as China. The two places in India that most interested the Romans were the ports of Barygaza and Muziris. Barygaza seems to have the busiest port of northwestern India, and the list of goods exported from Barygaza includes dyes, resins, cotton, and long pepper. Pepper was plentiful at Barygaza, but not cheap because of its distance from the pepper-producing regions of South India. At Barygaza, Romans exchanged wine (Italian wine was preferred, with Arabian wine in second place), copper, tin, glass and gold and silver for the long pepper and cloth they sought. Presumably, there was a resident Roman community here and there were references to the Romans maintaining storage facilities here. At the nearby port of Karachi, archaeologists have pulled Greco-Roman statues from the harbor and there is evidence of a Greek style temple.

Once the Romans figured out the monsoon system, probably in the first century C.E., they were able to sail directly to southern India to the port of Muziris. Muziris was in the heart of the black pepper production, and prices were correspondingly low compared to Barygaza. Ships came to Muziris from Arabia and from Roman Red Sea ports in great numbers. In exchange, the Romans brought silver coins and relatively small quantities of their usual trade goods—wine, glass, copper, and tin. The importance of Roman coin in this trade is attested to by the large number of coin hoards that have been found in southern India. There was no locally produced coinage at the time and Roman coins appear to have been widely used in commerce. The coins are often defaced, suggesting that they were used for their weight rather than as coins *per se.*

Pliny the Elder reports that convoys of as many as 120 Roman ships left the Red Sea annually for India, which means that Romans (largely Romanized Syrians) numbering in the thousands had some direct experience of India and points in between. It also meant that many more Romans who had never been to India had indirect knowledge of the land and its culture, although much of that knowledge was undoubtedly flawed and certainly incomplete. Our evidence for what the Indians knew about the Romans is exceedingly sketchy. There are a few references to efforts to bring the dharma

(Buddhist law) to the Yannas, as the Greeks and Romans were called, and two Indian diplomatic missions arrived in Rome during the first century, just as the Romans were beginning to make their presence felt in the Indian spice trade. The other interesting and little explored evidence of possible Roman cultural influence in India is the existence of Christian communities in India. The indigenous Christians of India call themselves St. Thomas Christians, in reference to the Apostle who is said to have traveled to India. We do not know how old these Christian communities are, and whether Christianity came by sea or overland through Persia, but their presence in India shows that India experienced some cultural influence as a result of these contacts between the Indian and Mediterranean Worlds. Some scholars suggest that Gnostic and neo-Platonic thought, which were part of the intellectual milieu of the Roman Empire and which influenced Christian theology, owe a deep debt to Indian religious ideas.

For the majority of Indians and Romans, however, the most intense encounter they had with each other was through the experience of each others' material culture. For people in the Mediterranean that meant the presence of pepper and other spices on the table or in their food. It meant using oils, ointments, cotton, and dyes that came from India. For Indians it meant Roman coins, glassware, and wine.

The Indianization of Southeast Asia

Before the first century boom in the spice trade, coastal Southeast Asia's cultures were evolving largely in isolation from the rest of Eurasia. But as the trade between China and India picked up, Southeast Asia was drawn into the larger narrative of Asian and world history.

There are two major ways of moving goods from the Indian Ocean to the South China Sea en route from India to China. One is overland across the Isthmus of Kra, the narrow point on the Malay Peninsula, and the other is by water through the Straits of Malacca (Map 1.1). In the first century, goods were brought by sea to the western side of the Isthmus of Kra and then carried overland to the eastern side. There they were put into ships again to finish the trip to China. Ships following this route passed by the mouth of the Mekong River, and before long a state known as Funan emerged there—the first known state in Southeast Asia. Its main port and emporium was Oc-eo, where merchants from China could buy Indian goods—especially pepper—and merchants from India could buy Chinese silk. Roman coins, as well as trade goods

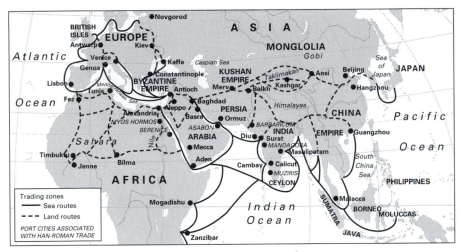

MAP 1.1   Port cities and trade routes of the spice trade.

from the Mediterranean, have been found there. The Romans themselves probably rarely ventured this far afield, but their coinage moved outside the range of their merchants.

By the third and fourth centuries C.E., Southeast Asia's place in the trading system was changing. Instead of just being an obstacle on the route between China and India, Southeast Asia was now a place where native entrepreneurs could sell local products to foreign merchants. For our purposes, the most important of these were cloves and nutmeg, though local gold was also an important commodity. Cloves and nutmeg from the islands of Indonesia, well to the south of Funan, were probably brought to the markets of Funan and even India by Malay sailors.

The Malay, natives of the Malay Peninsula, were master mariners, and Malay ships even made it as far as the East African coast, bringing several waves of settlers to the island of Madagascar beginning around 700 C.E. Madagascar is still inhabited by their descendants. Their maritime skills probably also enabled the Malays to open direct trade between the southern islands of the Indonesian archipelago and India, which had two significant consequences. One was a shift away from the Isthmus of Kra toward the Straits of Malacca. Ultimately this led to the decline of Funan and the rise of another state, Srivjaya, which was better situated to dominate the straits. The other effect, more cultural than political or economic, was the rising influence of India in the region.

Beginning in the second and third centuries, Indian religious ideas began to penetrate the court culture of Southeast Asia. How this happened is a bit of a mystery, but it seems likely that communities of Indian merchants arrived in Southeast Asia, and imported Brahmins, the priestly caste, to serve their religious needs. Brahmins then provided a critical mass of religious knowledge that lead to a widespread adoption of Hinduism by native Southeast Asian elites.

The putative role of Indians and Indian religious ideas in the creation of states in Southeast Asia is murky and contentious. At the very least, local state builders borrowed and adapted Indian models in order to lend themselves prestige and legitimacy. Whatever the role of Indians in the state-making process, it is clear that the spice trade brought them and their religions to Southeast Asia. By the seventh century, Buddhism and Hinduism were widespread in Southeast Asia, where they shaped the life of royal courts and, to a lesser extent, the lives of common people. Elaborate temples were erected, inscriptions in Sanskrit appeared, and Shiva Lingams (phallic representations of Shiva's creative power) became associated with royal authority. Southeast Asia also began to participate increasingly as a producer of trade goods—spices and scented woods—rather than just as a transit point for goods moving between India and China.

In this early period, the spice trade was very much trade in the sense used in the introductory chapter. Spices were high value, low bulk luxury goods that bound the various peoples of Eurasia to each other in a loose, but significant way. Because of the spice trade, the people of the Mediterranean had a rudimentary knowledge of Indian geography, a few people in India practiced a religion associated with the Mediterranean, and courts in Southeast Asia observed Indian religious practices, Chinese geographers had some knowledge of India and Southeast Asia, and coastal East Africa was drawn into the commercial and cultural orbit of the western Indian Ocean. However, there were real limits to this cross-cultural knowledge. Ptolemy (circa 85–165 C.E.), the greatest of the Greco-Roman geographers, did not include China on his maps, although the Romans did have a name for China—the land of the Seres, or silk producers—and knew that some of their favorite imports came from there, especially silk, known in Latin as *sericum*. Indians were exposed to some foreign merchants, but seem to have had little direct knowledge of the Mediterranean world. Southeast Asians practiced Indian religion but seem to have known little about India. It was an age of fleeting contacts where goods, especially high value ones like spices, moved farther across cultural lines than did people. The next major period in the Indian Ocean spice trade runs from 700 to 1500. During that time Islam became a critical factor in the commercial world of the Indian Ocean, and the Indian Ocean region went through a commercial revolution.

THE SPICE TRADE IN THE AGE OF ISLAM

Arab merchants had been active in the spice trade long before the rise of Islam. Their commercial networks extended to East Africa, India, and possibly, through a tenuous link, to China. As Islam spread through Arabia, it also spread through Arab trade networks. Thus, the conversion of the Arabs led to a minor Muslim presence in most of the ports of the Indian Ocean. The conversion of most Persians to Islam, a process that took several hundred years, but was mostly complete by 1000, furthered this process. Persian trade networks and those of their ethnic kin, the Sogdians, extended as far as China, so the conversion of Persia and Sogdiana (largely modern Uzbekistan) added to the numbers of Muslims moving along the spice routes of Asia.

Islam spread in two ways. The first and best known of these were the wars of conquest which began in the Caliphate of Umar (634–44) and concluded around 750, by which time Muslims were politically dominant from the Indus River to Spain. The lands of the Indian Ocean, the home of the spice trade, saw the occasional war of conquest by Muslims, but for the most part Islam spread through the Indian Ocean on the trade routes. Merchants performed their religious duty to proselytize, called *dawa*, and often found that their fellow merchants were interested in conversion.

From the merchant's perspective, Islam had much to offer. It is a universal religion. One can be as good a Muslim in Sumatra as in Arabia. Its founder, the Prophet Muhammad, was a merchant; thus, trade is an honorable profession. It has a single body of holy law— the Sharia—which applies to Muslims everywhere, and a contract between Muslims is enforced at opposite ends of the world in the same way. The Sharia also includes rules about fair trade, judicious use of weights and measures, and the proper treatment of coreligionists in trade. The centrality of the Arabic language to Muslim religious practice and scripture also meant that many Muslim merchants had at least a rudimentary knowledge of Arabic and thus a common commercial language. These factors, coupled with the growing economic power of the Muslim World, meant that there was a steady growth in the importance of Islam in the trade of Asia. The role of Muslims in trade became so pronounced that even in places ruled by non-Muslims the presence of Muslim merchants was not just tolerated but encouraged.

If the previous era of the Indian Ocean spice trade was shaped by the Han and Roman Empires, this one was initiated by the Abbasids and the Tang. The Abbasids (750–1258) were a Muslim dynasty of caliphs ruling from Baghdad that commanded the allegiance of most of the Islamic World. The Abbasid elite had as developed a taste for foreign luxuries, and Abbasid ports were busy with ships plying the sea routes that connected the Middle East, India, Africa, Southeast Asia, and China. Sindbad the merchant is of course a mythic character, but his stories come to us from Abbasid Baghdad, and he is supposed to have lived in the port city of Basra at the head of the Persian Gulf (other Arab cities, including Muscat, also claim Sindbad).

China, reunified by the short-lived Sui dynasty (589–618), experienced a new age of imperial expansion far into the western lands of Central Asia under the Tang dynasty (618–907). The Tang family was partially descended from Turkic nomads, and consequently its emperors—down to the mid-ninth-century—were unusually open to foreign ideas, influences, and trade. The imperial capital known as Chang'an (modern Xi'an) had a large community of resident foreign merchants, and annually welcomed thousands of merchants from a wide variety of lands, including Islamic regions far to the West. Likewise, Chinese merchants took up residence in the oasis towns of Tang China's western frontier, where they joined Sogdian and other merchants along the so-called Silk Road. Chinese maritime merchants also ventured abroad in greater numbers during the Tang period, often in their own ships. Chinese merchants became a significant presence in Southeast Asia, and Chinese ships began to show up in the ports on India's east coast.

The economic prosperity of these two empires provided a stimulus to the spice trade and, of course, other types of maritime trade too. By 1000, both empires were through. The Abbasids still existed, but their empire had shrunk considerably and even in the rump that was left they served mostly as figureheads for various Turkic groups who had seized power and kept the Abbasid caliphs around to lend religious legitimacy to their own governments. The Tang had fallen and were replaced by the Song (960–1279), another trade-friendly Chinese empire. But despite the fall of the Tang and severe weakening of the Abbasids, the tempo of commerce on the Indian Ocean continued to increase.

Between 1000 and 1500 the commerce of the Indian Ocean reached new heights. The volume of trade increased, the types of goods that moved long distances changed, and new port cities that were utterly dependant on trade emerged. Part of what made this possible was a technological revolution in shipbuilding. The ships that carried the trade of the Indian Ocean in the first half of the second millennium were bigger, faster, safer, and more efficient than earlier ships. They allowed for a whole different level and intensity to the trade of the Indian Ocean.

Specifically they played a role in the transition from trade to commerce. By about 1250 the sea lanes of the Indian Ocean were busy not just with high value goods, but also with bulky everyday goods. Rice and other grains, cotton cloth, and timber began to follow the same trade routes that had once been the exclusive domain of high value goods like spice. This also served to increase the volume of trade in high value goods. Spice and other luxury goods benefited from the growing prosperity of the region and from the greater volume of shipping. Some of the less valuable spices—pepper especially—began the transition from luxury goods to everyday commodity.

CROSS-CULTURAL INTERACTION IN THE AGE OF ISLAM

Perhaps the two most important cultural side effects of this booming commerce were the Islamization of Southeast Asia and East Africa and medieval Europe's growing knowledge of and interest in the spice trade. Just as trade networks brought Hinduism and Buddhism to Southeast Asia, trade also brought Islam to the same region. Muslim Indians and Arabs, who traveled to Southeast Asia for spices, carried with them their religion, as well as trade goods. Conversion began first in court and commercial circles, and involved many compromises. Alcohol, pork, and tattooing—all forbidden by Islam—were part of the social fabric of pre-Islamic Southeast Asia and were difficult to give up. One king famously decided to convert but then, upon learning that he would have to give up pork, decided to eat all his pigs and then convert. Despite these difficulties Islam, and especially the Sufi components of Islam, eventually became a fixture in Southeast Asian life.

Southeast Asia never fully converted to Islam. Most of mainland Southeast Asia remains Buddhist, with the exception of the Malay Peninsula which is mainly Muslim. It is in the islands of Indonesia that Islam is dominant, but even there the Islamization process is incomplete. The island of Bali remains home to a mixture of Buddhist and Hindu religious practices, and in many places hill people are still in the process of being converted from traditional animist faiths to either Islam or Christianity. That said, the process seems to have begun in the thirteenth century, and by the fifteenth century Islam was the standard religion of the major trading cities of the region.

Islam brought with it new forms of literacy. In addition to the Sanskritic writing systems that were introduced from India, there also seem to have been a number of indigenous scripts in Southeast Asia that were used for informal writing. Literacy in the scripts may have been fairly widespread, but the importance that Islam accords the written word, especially of the Arabic language, resulted in a transformation of literacy in the region. An Arabized form of Malay gradually became the standard language of Islamic trade in the region. Malay borrowed both vocabulary from Arabic and the Arabic script. The result was a cosmopolitan language and a cosmopolitan literature. Indeed, the advent of Islam and the spread of the Malay language and ethnic identity created an Islamic cultural tradition in Southeast Asia that transcended local tribal and kin loyalties.

In Europe, the changing nature of Indian Ocean trade did not go unnoticed. Spice had dropped out of the Western European (but not the Byzantine) diet after the fall of Rome. The crusades, which resulted in large number of western Europeans taking up residence in the Crusader States that were carved out of the Holy Land (1097–1291), taught Europeans about many things they had been missing. Sugar, the subject of Chapter 3, was one of the new commodities they were exposed to, and at the time it was considered a spice. They also learned about the other spices—pepper, cloves, cinnamon, and nutmeg. As crusaders returned to Europe, they brought with them their interest in spices, which then spread through the European aristocracy.

To meet this new demand, the Italians—especially the Venetians—deepened their trade relations with the rulers of Egypt. Muslim Egypt, which controlled the top of the Red Sea, also controlled most of the flow of spice between the Indian Ocean and Mediterranean. The Venetians negotiated the exclusive right to trade in spice with Egypt and were allowed to establish a *fondaco,* or residential trade outpost, in Alexandria. Each year a Venetian convoy left Alexandria with Europe's pepper supply. As monopolists, the Venetians could charge whatever the market would bear. Others noticed and were interested in obtaining access to this profitable trade.

Some Italians ventured beyond Alexandria and made their way to the source of the spice. Marco Polo (circa 1253–1324) is the most famous of medieval Italy's traveler-merchants, but by no means the only one. Most were more reticent than Polo about their travels either because they were not aware of the public's appetite for travel literature, or, more likely, because they considered their travels to be hard-earned trade secrets, not to be shared with others. Perhaps the most interesting of these was the fifteenth-century adventurer Nicolo de Conti, who traveled by himself through India and Southeast Asia, returning home through the Red Sea. When Conti got home told his story to Poggio Bracciolini, a humanist scholar with connections to the Vatican. Bracciolini, as was true of many Europeans of the time, was fascinated by "the Indies." He wrote and published a lengthy account of Conti's travels, which contains detailed and fairly accurate information about the culture and commerce of the Indian Ocean world.

By the end of the fifteenth century, the Indian Ocean was booming. Trade in spices, and other much more mundane goods, was commonplace. Islam had become a feature in the life of many, though not all, trading communities, and Europeans had been reconnected to the spice trade. For people in the Indian Ocean world the price of spices was dropping. Pepper was common and the fine spices increasingly so, but in Europe pepper remained expensive and the fine spices were rare and very expensive. Various groups of Europeans began to consider ways of getting direct access to the spice trade without having to submit to the Venetian/Egyptian monopoly.

EUROPEANS IN THE INDIAN OCEAN

In 1497, the Portuguese mariner Vasco da Gama left the Tagus with three ships and set out for India. His voyage around the Cape of Good Hope to Calicut in southern India was the culmination of nearly a century of Portuguese exploration in the Atlantic. In Calicut he was able, after much bluster and bullying, to buy a cargo of pepper. After an arduous return journey during which one of his ships had to be abandoned for want of a crew, he made it back to Lisbon with two ships laden with pepper. His arrival in Lisbon sent a shock through the spice trade. For the first time, Europeans had made direct contact with the spice markets of the Indian Ocean. Da Gama had subverted the Venetian–Egyptian spice monopoly and demonstrated that European ships could extend into the Indian Ocean.

In doing so he ushered in a new era in the spice trade, one with profound consequences for both Europeans and Asians. European states took a different view of trade and merchants than did Asian states. While some Asian states sought to encourage and facilitate trade, merchants and their affairs were generally considered a bit beneath the dignity of government. Merchant diasporas were generally ignored. When, for instance, the Chinese merchant community in Southeast Asia was abused by the Portuguese and then later by the Dutch, China did nothing. It was not considered to be part of the state's role to worry about such things. By contrast, European governments in the sixteenth century saw trade as a critical source of state wealth. While noblemen were still socially uncomfortable with merchants, they used the state's power to protect merchants abroad and to gain favorable terms of trade.

Da Gama's initial voyage was followed by regular Portuguese ventures into the Indian Ocean. These forays were not just about trade, they were also about commercial warfare. The second Portuguese voyage to India, led by Pedro Cabral, bombarded Calicut for two days. In 1510 the Portuguese captured the Indian port of Goa; by 1511 they had Malacca; by 1515 they had Hormuz, which controlled access to the Persian Gulf. In 1513 they tried to take Aden at the southwestern tip of the Arabian Peninsula, but failed. What they were trying to do was to control each of the critical trade circuits of the ocean. Although they did not take Aden, they were able to maintain partial control over the movement of ships between the Indian Ocean and the Red Sea. Using Goa as their headquarters, the Portuguese created the *Estado da India*, a commercial empire in the Indian Ocean. They sought to require that all ships trading on the Indian Ocean pay them a protection fee, for which they were granted a *cartaz*, or commercial passport. Ships stopped at sea or arriving in Portuguese-controlled ports without a *cartaz* were subject to confiscation. In short, the Portuguese were engaged in what amounted to state-sponsored piracy (Figure 1.2).

Why they chose this route is an interesting question. The Portuguese wanted access to the spice trade, but lacked the money to buy their way into the trade. Portugal was a small country and made nothing that was of interest to Asian consumers. What the Portuguese did have was military technology—which they were shrewd enough not to share—and ships. So they used their guns and ships to force

FIGURE 1.2   This drawing shows the important trading port of Malaca. Located on the western coast of the Malaysian peninsula, the city commanded a strategic position on the strait which shares its name. Given this location, the city grew rich via it's control over the main trade route linking the Indian Ocean to the South China Sea. The city was an important emporium for the trade of such items as nutmeg and mace, cloves, sandlewood, silk, cotton cloth, and tin. Not surprisingly, Malaca was also an important "melting pot" for Southeast Asian, Indian, Chinese, Islamic, and later European cultures.

Source: The Bridgeman Art Library International Ltd.

their way into the spice trade. By charging their Asian competition for the right to trade and by using their own ships to move goods within the Indian Ocean, the Portuguese were able to generate enough surplus that they could buy pepper and other spices and ship them back to Europe at a profit. In the sixteenth century they also had the ability to keep other Europeans out of the Indian Ocean.

The result was not total Portuguese dominance of the spice trade, but a strong Portuguese influence on maritime Asia. The *cartaz* system quickly became just another expense that Asian merchants had to work into their overhead, and the Portuguese eventually abandoned their efforts to exclude all Muslims from the trade. The Portuguese influence took many forms. The Portuguese presence in the Indian Ocean facilitated the Roman Catholic Church's missionary efforts in the region. Jesuits and Dominicans became a presence in many of the capitals of South and East Asia. Missionaries, who were often highly educated, served as a very different sort of cross-cultural broker than merchants. By mastering Chinese, Jesuits brought China its first exposure to western mathematics and science and the West its first translations of the Confucian classics.

Portuguese merchants and soldiers often moved well beyond the confines of Portugal's formal empire. Communities of Portuguese settlers formed in almost every trading port of the Indian Ocean. Many were Portuguese men who married local women—very few Portuguese women came out into the empire—and thus created what we call creole societies. These mixed communities, often a source of great worry to Portuguese political and religious authorities, used languages that mixed Portuguese with local tongues and similarly created architecture, clothing, and foods that mixed Portuguese and Asian elements. The Portuguese, despite the very limited nature of their empire, were instrumental in creating what historian Gregory Gunn has called the "First Globalization." Portuguese, he asserts, became the first global language used as a means of communication by English, Dutch, Chinese, Indian, African, and Malay merchants and officials. The movement of Portuguese ships and people played a critical role in spreading information between the various parts of Eurasia and the Americas. It forced Europeans and Asians to reconsider their place in the world and received knowledge from classical sources.

The other effect was to lower the price of spices in Europe. It was much cheaper to carry spices in big ships around the Cape than to move them up the Red Sea, then overland to the Mediterranean, and then back into ships. The result was the beginning of a shift in European consumption patterns. European spice use became more like that of Asia—more of an everyday item and less of a luxury. That the Portuguese were making good money at this was not lost on other Europeans, and eventually Portuguese supremacy in the Indian Ocean was challenged by the Dutch and the English.

In the late sixteenth century, Dutch ships began to appear in the Indian Ocean. Dutch sea captains came initially as privateers but by 1602 the *Vereenigde Oost-Indishe Compagnie* (known as the VOC) was created by the Dutch estates general in order to limit what they saw as destructive competition between various Dutch commercial interests in Asia. The VOC was a joint stock company, which means that it belonged to multiple private investors, each of whom had a financial interest in the company but left the management of the company to its directors. A similar company, the East India Company (EIC), was chartered in Britain with much the same purpose. Because these companies could have many investors, they had access to huge amounts of capital—far more capital than the state-controlled *Estado da India* could ever hope to muster. Their managers, cut from a very different cloth than the Portuguese noblemen who controlled the *Estado da India*, were bean counters at heart and ran their business with a ruthless efficiency that the Portuguese could not match. Though the Portuguese defended their commercial interests in the Indian Ocean with courage and tenacity, they were outgunned by the Dutch. It took until the middle of the seventeenth century, but over time the Dutch became the masters of the Indian Ocean's sea lanes.

The Dutch then set about the task of controlling the spice trade in a very different way than had the Portuguese, deciding they wanted to control not just shipping, but production. Pepper production was too widely distributed to be easily controlled—though the Dutch did seize the port of Cochin in an unsuccessful effort to monopolize the pepper trade, but fine spices were another matter. Cloves, nutmeg, and cinnamon came from fairly restricted places.

The case of nutmeg is instructive. In 1620 the Dutch conquered the island of Banda, virtually the only place where nutmeg was grown. They then cut off the rice supply to the island in order to depopulate it and brought in Dutch settlers and slaves to run the plantations. Through an act of genocide, the Dutch now controlled the world's nutmeg supply. It was not just Asians who bore the wrath of the VOC. An EIC trading post on the island of Amboina was captured and its English inhabitants tortured to death. The Dutch followed a similar, though somewhat less brutal, policy in the clove trade.

Eventually both the VOC and the EIC became territorial powers, with the Dutch controlling much of insular Southeast Asia and England's "John Company" ruling much of India. They marginalized the Portuguese because of their superior access to capital, their more efficient bureaucracies, and because, to a greater extent than the Portuguese, they were able to internalize their costs. The ability of both companies to move spice on a vast scale around the Cape to Europe resulted in a huge drop in prices. By 1750, spices were no longer the sort of thing that states went to war over, or which could be used to "justify" genocide. The companies had transformed the spice trade into commerce in spice.

SOURCES

Pepper and Cinnamon in the Roman World
Pliny the Elder, *Natural History*, Book XII

Gaius Plinius Secundus (23–79 C.E.), known as Pliny the Elder, was born into an elite Roman-Italian family and served the empire in several capacities. He commanded a cavalry squadron in Germany, studied law in Rome, was a procurator in Spain, and at the end of his life was commander of the fleet at Naples. His far-ranging interests covered the entire span of human knowledge, and his only extant work, the *Natural History*, deals with such diverse issues as how clouds are formed, the intelligence of dogs, and cures for an upset stomach. It also records his knowledge of the spice and silk trades. His knowledge of these trades was imperfect, but his accounts contain much that is factual and represent the state of Roman knowledge of Asia in the first century C.E.

As you read this document, keep the following issues and questions in mind. How accurate was Pliny's knowledge of the place of origin and types of pepper? What can you reasonably infer from your answer? What was Pliny's attitude regarding pepper? What might your answer suggest about the man and his worldview? What did Pliny know about cinnamon's place of origin? Compare it with his knowledge of pepper. What conclusions follow from your answers? Compare pepper and cinnamon's relative prices and uses in the Roman World of the first century C.E. What conclusions follow from your answers?

XIV   [T]rees resembling our junipers that bear pepper occur everywhere, although some writers have reported that they only grow on the southern face of the Caucusus.[1] The seeds differ from those of the juniper by being in small pods, like those which we see in the case of the kidney bean; these pods when plucked before they are open and dried in the sun produce what is called "long pepper," but if left to open gradually, when ripe they disclose white pepper, which if afterwards dried in the sun changes color and wrinkles up. Even these products, however, have their own special infirmity, and inclement weather shrivels them up and turns the seeds into barren husks, called *bregma*, which is an Indian word meaning "dead." Of all kinds of pepper this is the most pungent and the lightest, and it is pale in color.

Black pepper is more agreeable, but white pepper is of a milder flavour than either the black or the "long" pepper . . . It is easy to adulterate long pepper with Alexandrian mustard. Long pepper is sold at 15 denarii[2] a pound, white pepper at 7, and black at 4. It is remarkable that the use of pepper has come into so much favour, as in the case of some commodities their sweet taste has been an attraction, and in others their appearance, but pepper has nothing to recommend it in either fruit or berry. To think that its only pleasing quality is its pungency and that we will go all the way to India to get this! Who was the first person who was willing to try it on his viands, or in his greed for an appetite was not content merely to be hungry? Both pepper and ginger grow wild in their countries, and nevertheless they are bought by weight like gold or silver . . . Pepper is adulterated with juniper berries, which absorb its pungency in a remarkable manner, and in the matter of weight there are several ways of adulterating it.

XLII   In regard to cinnamonium[3] and cassia a fabulous story has been related by antiquity, and first of all by Herodotus,[4] that they are obtained from birds' nests, and particularly from that of the phoenix[5] . . . and that they are knocked down by the weight of the flesh brought up there by the birds themselves, or by means of arrows loaded with lead; and similarly there is a story of cassia growing round marshes under the protection of a terrible kind of bats that guard it with their claws, and of winged serpents—these tales having been invented by natives to raise the price of their commodities . . . cinnamonium, which is the same thing as cinnamon, grows in Ethiopia,[6] which is linked by intermarriage with the cave-dwellers (Troglodytes).[7] The latter buy it from their neighbors and convey it over the wide seas . . . to the harbor of the Gebbanitae[8] called Ocilia[9] . . . they say that it is almost five years before the traders return home and that many perish on the voyage. In return for their wares they bring back articles of glass and copper, clothing, and buckles, bracelets and necklaces; consequently that traffic depends on having the confidence of women . . . The right of controlling the sale of cinnamon is vested solely on the king of the Gebbanitae, who opens the market by public proclamation. The prices were formerly 1,000 denarii per pound, but this was raised to half as much again . . . His Majesty, Emperor Vespasian (r. 69–79 C.E.), was the first person to dedicate in the Temples of the Capitol and of Peace chaplets[10] of cinnamon surrounded with embossed gold. We once saw in the Temple of the Palatine erected in the honor of his late Majesty Augustus (63 B.C.E.–14 C.E.) by his consort

Augusta a very heavy cinnamon root placed in a golden bowl, out of which drops used to distill every year which hardened into grains . . .

Arab-Jewish Merchants in the Indian Ocean
Khalaf ben Isaac ben Bundar, *Letter*

The following letter was written by a Jewish merchant who lived in the port city of Aden (see the next source) in 1139. The letter's recipient was Abraham ben Yiju, probably the leading Jewish merchant in the south Indian town of Mangalore. Ben Yiju was originally from Tunisia, but had lived in Cairo and Aden before arriving in Mangalore.

The letter, along with thousands of others, was recovered from a *geniza*, or paper repository, at a synagogue in Cairo. Jews, forbidden to throw away any paper that had God's name on it, placed it in their synagogue's *geniza*. Because even the most informal letter or account book had some sort of invocation of the divine in it, a broad variety of texts ended up in *genizas*. This collection of letters, many of which focus on family matters or the day-to-day functioning of trade partnerships over long distances, offers a rare window into the lives of merchants.

The letters were written in colloquial Arabic (not the classical Arabic used by Muslim Arab writers) but with Hebrew rather than Arabic script. Judeo–Arabic, as this form of writing is called, demonstrates just how deeply embedded this Jewish community was in the larger Arab Muslim world in which it resided.

This particular letter deals with the details of running a business with branches on two sides of an ocean. As you read this document, keep the following questions in mind. What does the letter suggest about the relationship that bound Khalaf and ben Yiju? Based on this letter, how would you describe their business and the ways in which they conducted it? Three "slave agents" are mentioned in this text: Bama, who belongs to ben Yiju, Jawahar, and Bakhtyar. Bama is a South Indian name. The other two are Arab and Persian. What does this suggest about the Indian Ocean pepper trade? Look at the context in which these names are mentioned. What does this suggest about the status of these slave agents? Finally, in this book we have tried to look at various trades separately. Does this document suggest that we have oversimplified the process?

You mentioned, my master,[11] that you were longing for me. Believe me that I feel twice as strongly and even more than you have described; may God decree our coming together in the near future in complete happiness through his mercy, if God wills.

Shipments from India:

I took notice, my master, of your announcement of the sending of refurbished iron in the boat of nakhoda[12] Ibn Abi'l-Kata'ib. The shipment has arrived and I received from him two bahars[13] and one-third, as you noted.

The nakhoda Joseph arrived from Dahbattan[14] in the ship of Ibn al-Muqaddam and I received two basins, two ewers, and two basins for candle sticks from him . . .

As to the covers, which remained with you, my master, kindly send them. However, my lord, I have not received . . . the betel-nuts[15] mentioned by you, for you wrote that you sent them with Jawahar, the slave agent of Dafir, but he has not arrived this year.

Shipwreck:

As to your shipment, my master, forwarded from Fandarayana[16] in the ship of the Fatan Swami[17] through the Sheik Abu'l-Hasan b. Ja'far:

His smaller ship arrived and I took delivery from it of one and quarter and an eighth bahar of pepper, as was stated in your memo to my master, the illustrious elder Madmun,[18] as well as of a bahar of *amlas* iron.

The bigger ship, arrived near Berbera,[19] where its captain got into trouble with it until it was thrust against the Bab al Mandeb,[20] where it foundered. The pepper was lost completely; God did not save anything of it. As to the iron, mariners were brought from Aden who were engaged to dive for it and salvage it. They salvaged about one-half of the iron . . . All the expenses incurred for the diving and the transport will be deducted from whatever will be realized for that iron; the rest will be divided proportionally, each taking his proper share. I regret your losses very much . . .

Silk sent instead of gold:

I sent to you five mann[21] of good silk on my account, for I saw that my master, the illustrious Madmun, had sent some to Ben 'Adlan and to others and it was reported in his name that it is selling well in Malabar.[22] Therefore, I thought it was preferable to send, instead of gold, merchandise that might bring some profit. Thus kindly sell it for me for whatever price God, the exalted, apportions and grants, and buy me whatever God, the exalted, assigns and send it to me in any ship, without any responsibility for any risk on land or sea. If there is an opportunity to buy betel-nut or cardamom, kindly do so, but you, my master, need no instructions, for you are competent. Indeed, I cause you trouble every year; but, you, my master, do excuse me, as it has always been your habit, past and present.

Request to intervene with a Muslim notable:

Moreover, my master, last year, I sent to the captain Mas'ud, the Abyssinian,[23] 30 Egyptian mithqals,[24] to buy whatever God, the exalted, would apportion . . . He informed me that he had bought me two bahars of pepper, which he carried with him, and there remained for me 17¼ mithqals, which were deposited with my master, the illustrious Sheikh Abu 'l-Hasan 'Ali b. Ja'far.[25] Therefore, I, the captain Mas'ud, and Bakhtyar, the slave agent of 'Ali b. Ja'far, went to the illustrious Sheikh 'Ali b. Muhammad Nili, and he [Mas'ud] reported the matter to him, whereupon I received a notification from Nili to 'Ali b. Ja'far about it. When you meet him, kindly greet him for me and ask him to buy for me with this sum what God, the exalted, apportions and to send it on any ship without any responsibility for any risk on sea or land, in this world or the world to come. I do not need to give you instructions on how to approach him: *"a hint is sufficient for a wise man."*

Aden
Duarte Barbosa, *The Book of Duarte Barbosa*

Duarte Barbosa, Portuguese author of a detailed survey of the western Indian Ocean, lived in India from 1500 to 1516 or 1517, the early years of the Portuguese venture in South Asia. His uncle was the Portuguese factor, or financial agent, in Cananore, a port city in western India. Barbosa accompanied him as a scribe, and quickly acquired fluency in Malayalam, the language of southwest India. Later he and his uncle lived in Cochin, another western Indian trading port. Barbosa traveled widely and visited many of the ports about which he wrote. He seems to have returned to Europe because he felt he was unfairly passed over for promotion. Shortly after his return to Europe he joined his brother-in-law Ferdinand Magellan on his voyage of circumnavigation. Barbosa survived the crossing of the Pacific, but died in Sebu in the Philippines not long after Magellan's demise. His account was published in Italian in 1563.

The city of Aden, in modern Yemen, which he describes here, was one of the great trading emporia of its time. Its position at the entrance to the Red Sea allowed it to dominate trade between the Mediterranean and the Indian Ocean.

As you read this description of the city, keep the following questions in mind. What is the source of Aden's food supply? What does that suggest about the city and the nature of Indian Ocean trade in the sixteenth century? What do merchants come to buy at Aden? Where do these items come from? What does this tell you about Aden's role in the Indian Ocean? Spices were high on the list of trade goods that brought Europeans to the Indian Ocean. Judging from Barbosa's account how central to Indian Ocean trade were spices in the sixteenth century?

[W]e arrive at the wealthy and populous city of Aden, which belongs to the Moors[26] and has its own king. This city has a right good haven and an exceedingly great traffic in goods of importance. It is a fine town, with lofty houses of stone and mortar, flat-roofed, with many tall windows . . . The city is on a point between the mountains and the sea. The mountain is cut through on the mainland side, so that there is no way of going out save by one passage only which they can use; on no other side can they come in or go out.

The city has within it no water whatsoever, save that . . . there stands a great building to which they lead the water in pipes from the mountains a good way off . . . In this city are great merchants, Moors as well as Jews; they are white men and some of them black. Their clothing is of cotton, but some wear silk . . . Their food is excellent flesh-meat, wheaten bread and a great store of rice which come thither from India . . . To the harbor of this city come ships from all parts, more especially from the port of Juda,[27] whence they bring copper, quicksilver, vermillion, coral, and woolen and silken cloths, and they take thither on their return great store of spices and drugs, cotton cloths and other wares of the great kingdom of Cambaya[28] . . . They also take much woolen cloth, colored Meca[29] velvets, gold in ingots, coined and to be coined (and also some in strings), and camlets,[30] and it seems an impossible thing that they should use so much cotton cloth as these ships bring from Cambaya. They come to this city from Ormuz,[31] from Chaul, Dabul, Baticala, and from Calecut[32] (whence most of the spices are wont to come) with great store of rice, sugar, and coconuts; and many ships come also from Bengala, Camatra and Malaca,[33] which brings as well abundance of spices, drugs, silk, benzoin, lac, sanders-wood, aloes-wood, rhubarb in plenty, musk, thin Bengala cloths, and sugar (great store); so much that this place has a greater and richer trade than any other in the world, and also this trade is in the most valuable commodities.

Old Spices, New Knowledge
Garcia da Orta, *Colloquies in the Simples and Drugs of India: Cinnamon, Cloves, Mace and Nutmeg and Pepper*

Garcia da Orta (1499–1580) was a Portuguese apothecary and convert to Christianity from Judaism, who lived in Goa, the capital of the Portuguese empire in Asia. In 1563 he published an account of the various spices produced in Asia in the form of a dialogue between himself and a visitor from Europe named Ruano. Ruano's role was to present the current state of European knowledge about the origins and nature of the spices, Orta's was to correct him. In correcting Ruano, Orta often explicitly contradicted ancient authority—including Pliny. This extract is a good example of the role of cross-cultural trade in challenging received knowledge about the state of the world (Figure 1.3).

Please consider the following questions as you examine this document. What is Orta's attitude toward ancient authority? On what grounds does he overrule them? Reread Pliny's account of the origins of cinnamon. Is Orta's dismissal of Pliny's repetition of "a thousand fables" fair? In Orta's time the Portuguese tried to prevent pepper being shipped through the Red Sea because it would fall into the hands of Muslims. Was this working? Does Orta seem concerned about it?

Fifteenth Colloquy

Cinnamon

Ruano:

One cannot eat any spice with pleasure except cinnamon. It is true that the Germans and Flemings eat pepper, and here our negresses eat pepper, but Spaniards do not eat any of the spices except cinnamon . . . In place of what we call *cassia lignea*, the word *canela* is often used. It will be as well that we should discuss it now.

Orta:

Canela, and what we call Cassia Lignea, are one and the same thing: but the ancient writer saw this spice after it has come from such a

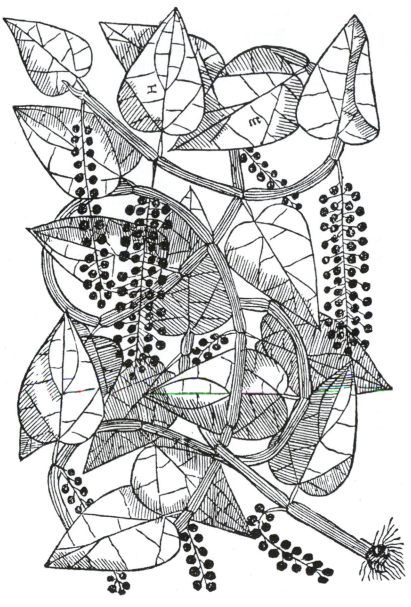

PLATE XX.—PIMIENTA.

FIGURE 1.3 This drawing comes from Garcia da Orta's, *Colloquies in the Simples and Drugs of India: Cinnamon, Cloves, Mace and Nutmeg and Pepper.* It show black pepper berries on the vine.

Source: Courtesy of Library of Congress.

distance that they could not have had a correct notice of it, and as the price was very high, there arose a thousand fables which Pliny and Herodotus repeat. They relate them as true, when in reality they are quite fabulous . . . The price being so high, and the avarice of men still higher, the drug was often falsified. As the false kind could never be exactly like the real kind in every respect, they made two kinds, one the true cinnamon and the other falsified one, both usually being of the same species. . . .

[A lengthy discussion of the distribution of cinnamon follows]

Ruano:

[In] the time of the Roman emperors, if a stick of true cinnamon was obtained it was considered a great treasure, so no wonder it was hard to get. It is said that in the time of Pope Paul[34] a piece was found which had been kept since the time of the Emperor Arcadius (r. 395–408 C.E.), and after 1,400 years there was great rejoicing.

Orta:

I will answer all this. I say that you can get more knowledge now from the Portuguese in one day than was known to the Romans after a hundred years. The stick which was given may have been brought from Lisbon, and would not have deteriorated. The piece belonging to the Emperor Arcadius may have been preserved by the will of God, or it may have been an imposture.

Forty-Sixth Colloquy

Pepper

Ruano:

I want you to tell me where the greatest quantity is grown, and the names of the countries where it is found . . . , how it is gathered, what the tree is like. . . .

Orta:

The greatest quantity of pepper is in Malabar, or along the coast from Cape Comorin to Cananore. There is also a certain amount in the parts of Malacca, which, however, is not so good, being less fruitful. There is some in Sunda and Java, and in Queda and other places, and it is consumed in China, in its own country, and is also taken to Martaban and Pegu. In Malabar also it is largely consumed in the country itself, where much more is used than in any other land . . . a large quantity goes to the Red Sea, against the orders of the king [of Portugal], but nothing can be so well guarded but that much will be taken westward by the Moors.

[Ruano asks about pepper production.]

Orta:

The tree of the pepper is planted at the foot of another tree, generally at the foot of a palm . . . It has a small root, and grows as its supporting tree grows, climbing round and embracing it. The leaves are not numerous, nor large, smaller than an orange leaf, green and sharp pointed, burning a little almost like betel. It grows in bunches like grapes, and only differs in the pepper being smaller in the grains, and the bunches being smaller, and always dry at the time that the pepper dries . . . In Malabar the plant is of two kinds, one being the black pepper and the other white; and besides these there is another in Bengal called the long pepper.[35]

Ruano:

It seems to me that you abolish all the writers, ancient and modern, by this that I have heard you say . . .

Orta:

In the first place, your worship must understand that pepper does not grow either on the skirt or on the slope of Mount Caucasus, as Pliny says . . . This you must know, for you know how far Mount Caucasus is from Malabar or Sumatra, places where there is the greatest quantity of pepper. Nor is it like juniper, for it is a climbing plant . . . This I know very well from the testimony of my eyes.

NOTES

1. The mountain range between the Black and Caspian Seas.
2. A denarius was a silver coin.
3. Cinnamon twigs.
4. A Greek historian of the fifth century B.C.E.
5. A bird from Egyptian mythology.
6. Not true, cinnamon grows in Sri Lanka.
7. A reference to either Somalia or South Arabia.
8. Probably the Qatabanians of modern-day Yemen.
9. A port near the Bab al Mandab, the entrance to the Red Sea.

10. Garlands, or wreaths.
11. A polite form of addres; the two men were social equals.
12. Ship's captain.
13. Bahar=300 pounds.
14. An Indian port.
15. The seed of the betel palm, a shrub of Southeast Asia; when chewed, it is a mild stimulant.
16. An Indian pepper port.
17. Chief merchant of an Indian town.
18. The leading figure in the Jewish community in Aden.
19. A Somali port.
20. Entrance to the Red Sea.
21. A standard 5 pound unit of silk.
22. The southwest coast of India.
23. An Ethiopian.
24. One mithqal equals 4.72 grams of gold.
25. His name suggests he was a Shia Muslim.
26. Technically, a Moor was a Muslim inhabitant of western North Africa, but here Barbosa uses it as a generic synonym for "Muslim."
27. Jiddah, the Red Sea port nearest to Mecca.
28. Cambay, the main port in the Indian region of Gujarat.
29. Mecca, the holy city of Islam in Arabia.
30. A rich cloth made of interwoven silk and camel or goat hair.
31. Hormuz, an island port at the entrance to the Persian Gulf.
32. Trade ports on the west coast of India.
33. Bengal, Sumatra, and Malacca.
34. Either Paul III (1534–1549) or Paul IV (1555–1559).
35. White pepper is not from a separate plant; it is decorticated black pepper. Compare Pliny's description of white pepper.

CHAPTER

2

The Salt Trade

INTRODUCTION: CHINA AND WEST AFRICA

Salt was important to agricultural societies everywhere, but we have chosen China and West Africa as case studies because they demonstrate how salt has influenced human societies in two radically different regions of the world. China is an excellent example of "temperate abundance," with rich soils and a benevolent climate that facilitated early adoption of sedentary agriculture and a subsequent early rise of organized political authority. Conversely, West Africa's environment, with its consistently warm climate, its tendency toward either too much or too little rain (depending on the season), and the generally poor quality of its soil, made extensive agriculture difficult. Yet, through skillful innovation, West Africans also were able to develop sedentary agriculture and large-scale political systems. As we shall see, societies in both areas were deeply influenced by the quest for, use of, and control of, salt—but often in very different ways.

SALT IN CHINA

China is a familiar topic for students of world history, for it is one of several societies that every world history textbook covers in detail. In part, this is because of China's profound influence on its neighbors. Moreover, China's extensive written record and its system of a clearly defined political hierarchy have tended to make Chinese history a comfortably familiar area of inquiry for Western audiences. Further, China has long been a source of products the West wanted, such as silk and porcelain, and long-distance trade in these items has attracted considerable historical attention. In this chapter, however, we will study Chinese history in a different way. We will look at salt, a common product mass-produced in China for local consumption, and then examine how a simple commodity could be so deeply enmeshed in China's social, economic, and political systems.

Timeline of Chinese History

circa 2100–circa 1600 B.C.E. Xia Dynasty?

1700–1027 B.C.E. Shang Dynasty
1027–771 B.C.E. (Western) Zhou Dynasty
770–221 B.C.E. (Eastern) Zhou/Spring & Autumn Period/Era of Warring States
221–207 B.C.E. Qin Dynasty (China "unified")
202 B.C.E.–220 C.E. Han Dynasty
220–589 C.E. Three Kingdoms/Western & Eastern Jin/Southern & Northern Dynasties (breakdown of unified Chinese administration)
581–618 C.E. Sui Dynasty (China Reunified, in 589)
618–907 C.E. Tang Dynasty
907–960 C.E. "Five Dynasties"
960–1279 C.E. Song Dynasty
1279–1368 C.E. Yuan Dynasty
1368–1644 C.E. Ming Dynasty

1644–1911 C.E. Qing Dynasty

China was one of the first parts of the world to develop sedentary agriculture. As early as 5000 B.C.E. there were village communities in the regions of the Yellow and Yangzi river valleys that lived off diets largely consisting of millet and rice, respectively. As such, these proto-Chinese developed an early need for, and appreciation of, salt. A traditional Chinese children's song identifies the seven necessities of daily life as "firewood, rice, oil, salt, soy sauce, vinegar, and tea." Given that salt is a key ingredient in soy sauce, it is not entirely unreasonable to say that salt occupies two of the seven categories. Further, salt is not only a seasoning (a role often played via soy sauce), it is also a crucial component in the pickling of vegetables, eggs, and other foodstuffs for storage.

CHINESE SALT PRODUCTION

Of course, to use salt, one has to get salt, and the origins of salt production in China appear to extend back over 4000 years. Archaeological evidence from northwestern China suggests that local inhabitants were using the technique of boiling to extract salt from brine lakes as early as the third millennium (2000s) B.C.E.. In the region of Shansi and Shensi provinces, salt was sometimes even collected from evaporated lakebeds in the dry season. Inhabitants also learned to divert water from salt lakes into shallow holding pools, allowing the water to evaporate over a period of months. The natural salts would then be collected. Deposits of several million round-bottomed ceramic pots found in Sichuan Province in southwestern China suggest an organized system of salt-processing by boiling during the same period. Scholars believe that the salt was then traded down the Yangzi River to the salt-poor regions of Hubei and Hunan. Similarly, evidence suggests that sometime prior to 2000 B.C.E. salt also began to be extracted directly from seawater. Over time, the coastal regions became the center of Chinese salt production, eventually providing roughly 80 percent of China's annual salt output. By the fourteenth century C.E., China would produce over *500 million pounds* of salt a year.

The process of producing edible salt is not as simple as it might immediately appear. If one were simply to take seawater and boil it down, the return on the investment of labor and fuel would be quite poor. As a result, the early Chinese developed and gradually refined a process by which the salinity of the seawater was concentrated. Similar processes were often necessary for the water from inland salt lakes and brine wells.

The techniques for concentrating brine often involved a number of complex stages. The most common technique involved the use of ashes from either reeds or rice straws to absorb the salt and help to evaporate the water. Thus, a large area could be prepared with a thin layer of ash, and then repeatedly sprinkled with seawater or brine over the space of several days or even weeks. Only when the ashes had absorbed an adequate amount of salt would a much greater quantity of seawater or brine be leached through the ashes, strained into a collection pit, and then transferred or transported for boiling. To do this effectively required the construction of sheltered, watertight leaching basins and the careful channeling of the salt water, often from long distances.

This complex process is discussed in detail in a text called the *Aobo Tu*, written in the early fourteenth century C.E. by Chen Chun, who worked as a civil servant in the salt ministry of the Yuan dynasty. Chen Chun provides us with a detailed account of salt production— combining prose, poetry, and illustrations to describe each of the 47 steps necessary to produce salt from seawater. Careful timing was critical to many steps of the process. For example, the leaching process had to finish in time for the annual high tides that were necessary to channel the large quantities of seawater through prepared canals to the leaching fields. The techniques described by Chen Chun likely represent a refinement of a process that had been used on the Chinese coast since around 2000 B.C.E.. Excerpts from Chen Chun's book can be found at the end of this chapter.

Once the brine was sufficiently concentrated, the next step was to boil it down to yield salt. Early Chinese techniques for boiling brine employed small ceramic pots. By Chen Chun's time, however, the system had shifted to the use of large iron pans (up to ten feet in diameter). Chen Chun suggests that iron-poor areas relied on large ceramic or oyster-shell lime pans formed around a woven frame, but such pans had to be replaced after a matter of days, while iron pans could serve for months or even sometimes years. The boiling of seawater or brine yielded two types of salt. The most common, known as *lua-yen* (crystal salt), was extracted before the water was completely boiled away and had a pure white granular consistency. The other, *pa-yen* (cake salt), extracted only after the water had boiled away, was darker and formed a solid block. *Pa-yen* was considered to have a finer taste and generally commanded a higher price.

Chen Chun provides a detailed and sympathetic description of the nature and organization of the labor undertaken by the salt workers under his direction and states in his preface, "Those who have in mind to love the people will be moved by these [descriptions and] illustrations and they will certainly be able to devise excellent policies to improve the livelihood of the people." From his description we can identify several elements of the labor process involved in producing salt. First, the basic unit of production was the household. Individual families in salt-producing regions were required to produce a quota of salt each year, which was in effect an annual tax on people's time and labor over a period of several weeks. Everyone, regardless of age or sex, was expected to pitch in, probably because the process involved several time-sensitive procedures that required everyone to contribute as much labor as possible. Further, the relative wealth of the families could vary considerably. Chen Chun's illustrations show that some families could employ large wheeled carts to transport materials and fuel, while others had to use simple (and painfully inefficient) sledges. For certain tasks, such as the digging of channels to transport seawater to the leaching basins, organized communal labor was necessary.

Until around the third century c.e., the process of boiling and refining salt from landlocked Sichuan's brine-springs was probably similar to that described over one thousand years later by Chen Chun. However, in 252 b.c.e., a local administrator named Li Bing ordered the digging of wells to access new sources of underground brine. Some of these early wells reached depths of 100 meters. While this was a remarkable endeavor, which allowed this interior region to greatly expand its salt production, it was to serve as an intermediary step toward an even more remarkable innovation. In the process of digging the brine wells, it was noted that workers sometimes died for no apparent reason. Similarly, birds flying over the wells occasionally dropped dead. The cause, not immediately understood, was that the wells were not only hitting brine deposits, they were also releasing natural gas. Over the next 400 years, the local workers and inhabitants discovered that flames could be lit around such wells and that they would burn for a very long time, if not indefinitely. By the third century c.e., local salt producers had figured out how to channel the gas produced from these wells using pipes made of bamboo, and were using the gas to boil the brine extracted from the wells to make salt! This was a startling technological achievement, and is really without parallel elsewhere in the world at the time—or for centuries to follow. Improved drilling techniques would, over several hundred years, eventually replace the digging of wells, and allowed sources of brine and gas to be tapped at depths of down to 1,000 meters. Drilling to such a depth could take years, but the payoff could be significant. Some of the gas wells provided enough fuel to serve hundreds of salt-boilers at a single time, and networks of bamboo pipes up to 300 meters long were used to channel the gas a safe distance from the boreholes. Some of the wells produced not gas but crude oil, which was used as a medicine more often than as a fuel. Remarkably, the Sichuan salt-gas works were so successful that they remained in production well into the twentieth century.

SALT AND GOVERNMENTAL POWER

Given the increasing scope and value of salt production in China, it can hardly be a surprise that it drew the interest of the region's ruling classes from the earliest days. Legend has it that the quasi-mythical King Yu of the Xia dynasty ordained that the region of Shandong on the northeastern coast would provide salt to the government. The Xia, about whom we know very little, were succeeded by the Shang dynasty, which ruled the region around the Yellow River from roughly 1750 to about 1040 B.C.E.. While the Shang based much of their power on their control of bronze, which gave them a monopoly over bronze weapons and chariots, there is evidence that the state also became involved in the production and trade of salt. By the twelfth century B.C.E., the Shang held a monopoly over the production of salt from inland salt ponds. Porters delivering the salt became known as "people from Shang," and eventually "Shang people" became a term applied to all who worked in state-controlled industries.

Beginning in the late twelfth century B.C.E., a new dynasty rose to power in China. Known as the Zhou, this new state expanded far beyond the boundaries of the Shang, especially to the south. In part because of its size, and also because the rise of widespread iron-working technology ended the royal monopoly on deadly force, the Zhou dynasty was far more decentralized than the Shang. In the eighth century B.C.E., invasions of pastoralists from the north overran much of the region, and forced the Zhou to relocate their capital farther to the east. Sometime during this period, the semi-independent region of Qi, located on the Shandong peninsula, established the first formal state monopoly over the production and distribution of salt. Some historians believe this took place as early as the seventh century B.C.E., but the only written account of this policy appears to have been authored during the third century B.C.E.. Either way, the monopoly, which included the production of iron as well as salt, was appealing to those in power, in no small part because it provided the government with the funds necessary to create a formidable standing army.

Indeed, the monopoly on salt and iron became a recurring (perhaps even dominant) principle of Chinese government and administration. China was first unified under the Qin dynasty in 221 B.C.E.. Though it lasted only until 206 B.C.E., the Qin Empire set the precedent for a unified China that predominated to the present. The new state was ruled through a philosophy known as Legalism, which focused on the all-encompassing power of the state and condemned the corrupting influence of commercial competition. The monopoly on salt and iron was well suited to such an ideology, since it restricted public access to these lucrative areas of production and provided the state with funds to maintain its considerable military. As such, the monopoly was energetically embraced by the Qin and extended throughout the empire.

When the Qin Empire collapsed in 206 B.C.E., it was replaced by the much longer-lived Han Empire (202 B.C.E. to 220 C.E.). The Han, for the most part, embraced the kinder, gentler philosophy of Confucianism in place of Legalism, which stresses the importance of benevolence rather than force as a means of maintaining order and creating prosperity. As such, the Han initially ended the monopoly over salt and iron. However, by 120 B.C.E. the government was faced with fiscal shortfalls, in no small part because of the expense of conflict on the empire's northern border with the semi-nomadic Xiongnu. In response, the state reestablished the monopolies over salt and iron, and added one on wine and beer. Not too surprisingly, they promptly saw a considerable increase in state revenues. This remained the case until 81 B.C.E. when a faction of Confucian scholars at the court convinced the new Emperor Zhao (who was only in his teens) to call for a formal debate over the continuation of the monopolies. Reportedly some 60 scholars were invited to the court to debate the issue, with clear lines drawn between those who felt the monopoly was good and proper (thus displaying Legalist tendencies) and the Confucian scholars who saw it as counterproductive.

The resulting debate was recorded in the form of *The Discourses on Salt and Iron*, which has survived to this day (although many believe it was later edited to make the Confucian scholars look extra smart), and excerpts of it are included at the end of this chapter. The format of the *Discourses* is framed as a debate between "the Lord Grand Secretary" (who represents the pro-monopoly faction) and "the Literati" (who oppose the monopoly). The debate, which revolved around whether the demands of finance justified state control over the economy, was far ranging. *The Discourses* contains frequent references to ancient Chinese mythology, and its recurring metaphor is that the economy is a human body and the government is a physician attending to its health. In the end, the state opted to end only the monopoly on wine and beer, maintaining control over salt and iron. The monopolies were ended briefly in 44 B.C.E., but were reinstated again in 41 B.C.E.. In the late first century C.E., the monopolies were again abolished, and remained so for a period of several hundred years, not being reestablished until the rise of the Tang Empire in 618 B.C.E.. Once reestablished by the Tang, they played a dominant role in the Chinese economy until the collapse of the Qing Dynasty in 1911.

Chinese writing uses both pictographic and ideographic symbols to convey meaning. That is, each character is either a picture of a thing or a concept. These two characters represent the growing Chinese involvement in salt production. Both mean "Salt," but the earlier character, probably dating from the Shang Dynasty, is a straightforward pictographic representation of a salt pan or drying field. The second character is a more complex ideographic representation, the salt attended by an "imperial agent" (denoted by a figure with a coat-tail). By showing the salt accompanied by the Chinese bureaucrat, the image implies that salt and the government are inseparable. This latter character, in use by Han times, remained in common usage into the twentieth century, and demonstates the importance of salt to the Chinese state.

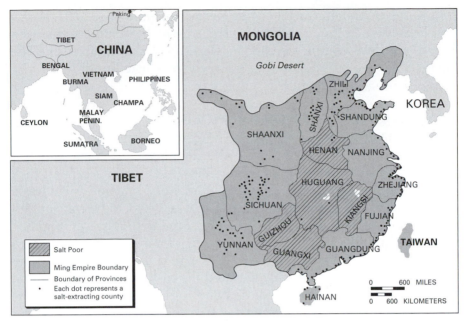

MAP 2.1   Sources of salt in Ming China, 1368–1644.

Indeed, salt would generally provide over half and sometimes as much as 80 percent of all Chinese government revenues (Map 2.1). By the time of the Ming (1368–1644 C.E.) and Qing (1644–1911 C.E.) empires, the government had developed intricate systems for the control of salt production and distribution. Beginning in 1370, the Ming government administered the salt monopoly through the "Certificate System." Under this arrangement, each salt-producing household was required to provide an annual quota of salt to the government (see the excerpt from the *Aobo Tu* at the end of this chapter). In return the household was provided with a fixed payment to cover wages and expenses. The salt was then transported to one of over two hundred official salt depots, which were located within 15 salt administration regions. Salt merchants, for their part, received certificates giving them the right to transport and market salt from the government depots, but only after they had delivered grain to garrisons serving on the northern frontier. This replaced the previous system, used by the Yuan Dynasty, wherein merchants bid for the right to distribute salt. Thus, the Ming government guaranteed a supply of food for troops through the monopoly on salt. Salt was then delivered to local retailers and sold to the public. In the late Ming period, beginning in 1631, a new process known as the "Syndicate System," which eventually created a hereditary class of salt merchants, placed salt distribution into the hands of a small group of families. This system lasted until 1831.

CONSEQUENCES OF THE SALT MONOPOLY

While both the Certificate and the Syndicate systems directed considerable amounts of money into the government's coffers, they had significant drawbacks. First, the mandatory system of wholesale depots run by the government meant that salt had to be transported long distances even when there was a local market. Thus salt might be produced in a region, transported to a depot far away, and then return in the hands of licensed merchants to be sold to the public by local retailers. Such a process greatly elevated the cost of salt to the common buyer, and created a substantial demand for smuggling and even the raiding of salt caravans. It is estimated that anywhere from one-quarter to one-half of the salt consumed during the Ming and Qing periods was manufactured and sold on the black market outside of state control, despite the continued efforts of the state to restrict such activities.

In a fine example of historical continuity, these issues were exactly the problems debated in the *Discourses on Salt and Iron*. The state derived considerable revenue from the control of salt, but it did so at the expense of the workers, who not only had to provide labor to the government, but who also paid elevated prices for a daily necessity of life. In turn, the people resisted the government's control over salt by creating an underground economy in smuggled and stolen salt. In effect, the state encouraged the populace to undertake an illegal trade in salt. Thus, despite the official dominance of Confucian thought in Chinese administration, the reality of fiscal necessity encouraged a series of Chinese governments to maintain a policy established by Legalist thinkers well over two thousand years before.

SALT IN WEST AFRICA

Unlike China, the region of West Africa has only recently begun to receive serious attention from world historians. Simply put, West Africa does not have as rich a written record as China. Similarly, the political systems developed by West Africans did not tend toward highly centralized and vertically organized bureaucracies, and as such often seem "foreign" to historians. Doing African history requires our using new historical techniques (such as examining oral histories and using sources such as linguistics and archaeology) and framing new questions that might throw light on systems of political organization that are unfamiliar to western-trained researchers. Perhaps more importantly, scholars also have had to overcome a legacy of racism that advocated an image of Africa as ahistorical—a land and people without change or development.

Thankfully, the development of African history has helped to reconstruct the history of Africa and Africans. Indeed, one of the favorite topics of African (and world) historians has been the empires of Ghana, Mali, and Songhai, which dominated the politics and economics of the savannah (grasslands) region of West Africa from the middle of the first millennium c.e. to the end of the sixteenth century. A dominant theme of these works has been the role of the trans-Saharan trade in gold in making these empires among the wealthiest in the world during their time. And there is no doubt that gold was important to the savannah states (and to Europe and the Middle East). However, this section will examine not gold, but salt, in the history of the West African savannahs. Gold was certainly a source of profit, but salt was a necessity of life. As such, the process of acquiring and producing salt played a profound role in influencing the development of the history of the West African savannahs.

Like China, the West African savannahs were the locus of considerable human innovation in agriculture. As early as 5000 B.C.E., sorghum and millet were domesticated in the region. The soils of the African savannahs, however, are relatively infertile and are notoriously fragile. Because they were unable to sustain repeated plantings, the ability of West African farmers to produce enough surplus to support large cities was restricted, and such urban centers did not become common until the early first millennium c.e..

West Africa's Sources of Salt

A number of sources of salt were initially drawn upon to meet the demand created by the Savannah's growing population of farmers and city dwellers. Trade with pastoralists who herded goats and cattle in the region provided a certain amount of salt simply by way of the intake of meat, blood, and dairy products. Some salts, many of them natrons (sodium carbonate and sodium sulphate), were collected from the dry basins of lakes that formed during the rainy months of May through September, and dried up in the dry season. Sea salt appears to have also been used early in West African history. An excavation at Zounbodje, in the modern nation of Benin, uncovered the remains of an extensive sea saltworks dating to the seventh century C.E.. Here, small clay pots were used to boil down seawater, and while they certainly produced salt for the local forest-dwelling population, the quantities produced suggest that export may have stretched far inland toward the savannahs. Similar works in the region of the Senegambia in the seventeenth century supplied salt to urban centers up to 1,000 kilometers inland, using the natural trade routes of the Senegal, Gambia, and Niger rivers. In many regions of West Africa, local populations produced salt from vegetation. For example, in the inland Niger Delta area of modern Nigeria, red and white mangrove trees were cut and burned. The ashes were then leached to produce highly concentrated brine, which could be boiled to produce salt and which was traded north up the Niger River. Even in fairly arid regions far from the sea, such as Fog'la in Chad, burning certain varieties of brush could produce ash from which to extract salt. But the high labor input demanded by this process meant that it was generally only used when salt could not be acquired through any other means.

For the urban areas of the Savannah a source of salt became increasingly available around the third century C.E., when the introduction of the dromedary (single-humped Arabian camel) to the Saharan region greatly facilitated the movement of heavy goods across the Sahara Desert. Thus, while there had been some degree of trade across the Sahara for over a thousand years, the earlier reliance on oxen and donkeys for animal traction placed a considerable limit on the scope of this trade because neither animal was able to travel long distances without water, and they were also poorly suited to travel across soft desert sands, into which their hooves were all-too-prone to sink. As such, trade was limited, and tended to take the form of goods being passed from oasis to oasis, often changing hands many times along the way—greatly increasing the costs of the products as they moved. Camels, of course, are well adapted to desert environments, being able to walk over soft sand, endure sandstorms, go days without water, and eat almost anything (Figure 2.1). Also, camels are quite

FIGURE 2.1 This photograph from the 1930s shows the arrival of a salt caravan in the city of Timbuktu.

Source: Peter Arnold, Inc.

strong, with healthy animals being able to carry up to 400 kilograms (880 lbs) of goods, though a standard long-range load for a camel is usually around 150 kilograms (330 lbs). With camels, trade could take the form of direct transport across the desert, with large caravans proceeding across the desert with stops only to replenish water and food supplies at known oases. Such a trip could still take months, but it was now possible to move considerable quantities of goods between the North African coast and West African Savannah.

Thus, the early centuries c.e. saw both the independent urbanization of the West African Savannah along the Niger River, and the introduction of the camel to the region. Together, these two factors created the demand for, and means of, expanded trans-Saharan transport. The goods that made up this new trade took many forms. North African cloth, spices, and finished goods might be traded for ivory and other animal products from the savannah region, for example. Trade in slaves also moved in both directions across the desert (having slaves from distant lands was an important marker of status, and showed the cosmopolitan worldliness of political and economic elites on both sides of the Sahara). Perhaps most important was the flow of gold northward from the forest regions of West Africa, across the savannahs and desert, to North Africa, where it might be minted or traded abroad to Europe or the Middle East. Indeed, prior to the discovery of the Americas, West Africa was the primary source of the gold circulating in the Mediterranean world.

Coming from the regions of the northwestern Sahara was high-quality salt that originated from huge desert salt pans—a legacy of the Sahara's once moist past. Thousands of years before, the region of the Sahara had been well watered, but long-term environmental change led to the gradual drying of the region's once massive lakes. The saltpans left behind were often many meters deep and covered hundreds of square miles—there for the taking. The value of the salt was astronomical, but so were the challenges of getting it out of the ground in the middle of the desert and transporting it over hundreds of kilometers of desert to the markets of the savannah. Camels solved this problem, by allowing the importation of food (and often water) to the saltpans to feed laborers (usually slaves) and then transportation of the salt south. Not only was this salt of high value, but its tendency to form hard slabs greatly facilitated transport. Each camel carried two slabs, one on each side. So valuable was this salt in the Savannah, that the costs of extraction and transport were easily recovered. Similarly, merchants could use the salt to purchase goods (such as gold or ivory) that were more valuable in the north than the south. Thus, profits could be acquired in each direction.

The Structure of the Trade

While we know that the volume of trans-Saharan trade increased rapidly after the arrival of the camel, we know little about what form this trade took in the early centuries of its existence because of the absence of any written record for this early period and the fact that such trade leaves little or no archaeological "footprint." Salt and gold were generally too valuable for people to leave lying around, and because the extraction of each took place in deserts and forests far from regions of concentrated human settlement, reconstructing their production in antiquity is difficult at best. Our current best evidence is the testimony of Arab geographers, who recorded accounts of trade with the savannah states, and these accounts do not begin until after the advent of Islam resulted in the "Arabization" of North Africa in the seventh and eighth centuries c.e.. Excerpts from two of these sources are included in the documents section at the end of this chapter.

The earliest records of the trade are fairly sketchy, are certainly secondhand, and reflect as much myth and ignorance about the savannahs and their inhabitants as what is likely accurate historical information. For example, several early Arab writers, such as Ibn al-Fiqih, made reference to the fact that gold actually grew in the ground of the savannahs "like carrots," and was plucked from the soil every morning by the local inhabitants. This is obviously incorrect, but these same geographers somehow manage to accurately describe the diet of the local inhabitants, stating that they ate sorghum, millet, and cowpeas. The explanation for this apparent inconsistency is fairly simple. Because the gold came from the forest regions south of the savannahs, the Berber and Arab traders from whom the scholars received their information did not themselves know where the gold came from or how it was extracted—just that there was a lot of it in the savannahs. Hence, the explanations given were a bit on the fanciful side. On the other hand, these traders made accurate observations of local lives.

The scholars also consistently reported that there was an increasing demand for salt in the growing urban centers of the Savannah. Early descriptions of what is often called "silent trade" between Berber or Arab merchants and West Africans describe an exchange between communities who apparently had no language in common. Merchants from the north would lay out their trade goods (often including salt), and retreat out of sight. Local traders would then approach, measure out a quantity of gold next to the trade goods, and themselves retire. If the northern traders found the amount of gold acceptable, they would take it and leave, if not, they would once again move out of sight. Such silent bargaining reputedly took place until an equitable exchange was reached, and one trader or the other picked up the offered items and left. If such a system did exist, it was later supplanted by a face-to-face trade of considerably greater volume and government regulation.

As the savannah states grew in size and power from the ninth through sixteenth centuries c.e., the demand for salt from the desert grew proportionately, and as the volume of this trade expanded, so did the accuracy of the accounts recorded by Arab geographers. Al-Bakri, writing in the eleventh century, provides a detailed account of the capital of Ancient Ghana. Indeed, he describes an entire town inhabited by Muslims that adjoined the local capital. He also makes it clear that Ancient Ghana was not only importing salt from the desert for consumption, it was also re-exporting it to other regions of West Africa—and reaping wealth from taxing the salt when it entered and exited the country. While many historians have correctly stressed that Ghana gained wealth from gold, they seem to overlook the fact that control over trade in salt was also a source of wealth for this state. Indeed, it is likely that salt was of greater value to the savannah states than gold. As with silk from China, Western historians have tended to focus on the importance of goods imported into Europe. But, as with China, salt was likely the single most important commodity for the economic health of the cities and states of the Savannah. Clearly, the growing wealth of the savannah states was a considerable factor in their physical expansion and power. Ghana ruled the western Sudan region along the Niger River from roughly the third century c.e. to the twelfth. Ancient Mali, more of a trading empire than a state, controlled a region stretching from the Atlantic Ocean to modern-day Niger from the thirteenth through the fifteenth century. Another empire, Songhai, ruled over an area that extended from the eastern borders of the Senegambia to Northern Nigeria from the early fifteenth through the late sixteenth century. Notably, Songhai even extended its power northward to seize several important Saharan salt mines, further expanding its degree of control over this important monopoly.

By the fourteenth century we have highly detailed and accurate accounts of trade and life in the savannahs. Indeed, some of the accounts are firsthand, rather than hearsay. For example, Ibn Battuta, a Moroccan writer who was perhaps the best-recorded traveler of the pre-modern world, journeyed extensively in the savannahs, and recorded his experiences in great detail. Excerpts of his accounts of the salt mines of Teghaza and the urban centers of Ancient Mali are found at the end of this chapter.

Salt and Cultural Change in the Savannahs

The expanding trade between the savannahs and North Africa, however, was not simply in items such as salt, gold, and ivory. Culture, too, was being exchanged between these regions—however unintentionally. Perhaps the most significant aspect of this exchange was the introduction of Islam into the urban regions of the West African savannahs. Such an outcome is not surprising. One of the more significant grand narratives of world history over the past two thousand years has been the spread of world religions—religions that seek to convert others to their systems of belief. By and large, world religions (also often called "salvation religions") such as Buddhism and Christianity, have successfully expanded into regions where peoples previously practiced more locally focused pantheistic religions. Islam, too, encourages its adherents to proselytize. There can be little doubt that the Arab and Berber Muslims who traveled to the savannahs felt obligated to spread the message of Islam. Similarly, it is clear that they met with gradual but nonetheless increasingly significant success—particularly among local political and economic elites. This could be because these elites spent more time interacting with Muslim traders, and thus had more time to be swayed. From another perspective, it could be that these elites' increasingly cosmopolitan outlook encouraged the adoption of a religion that explained not the local, but rather the global human community. By the eleventh century, Arab writers were noting that the rulers of such savannah kingdoms as Takrur and Ghana had converted to Islam.

The pilgrimage to Mecca of the Malian ruler Mansa Musa in 1324–1325 reflects the growing influence of Islam among the region's ruling classes. His investment in Islamic education and the building of mosques did much to help turn Mali (particularly Timbuktu) into a major center of Islamic scholarship. Furthermore, prolific spending of gold during his visit to Egypt and the Hejaz (the Islamic holy land in western Arabia) likely did much to convince Muslims in the Middle East that West Africans were devout (and wealthy) Muslims. Indeed, by the sixteenth and seventeenth centuries, so many Africans in the savannah regions had converted to Islam that Muslims elsewhere included the region as part of the *Dar al-Islam* (Home of Islam), rather than referring to it, as they had previously, as *Dar al-Sudan* (Home of the Blacks). In 1655 the scholar Al-Sa'di noted in passing that "Jenne is one of the greatest markets of the Muslim world. There the salt merchants of Teghaza meet merchants carrying gold from the mines of Bitou."

It is important to note that the integration of foreign cultural elements is always a complex process. West African Muslims did not simply cast aside their traditional religions and ways of life and accept Islam as a unit of belief and practice. Rather, they embraced those aspects of Islam that they found most appealing and maintained elements of local religious and social culture they considered important. West African Muslims, much to the dismay of observers such as Ibn Battuta, were far less eager to restrict women's social mobility than did their contemporary North African counterparts. This blending of indigenous West African elements with Islam—a phenomenon called "syncretism"—has even led to creation of a religion known as *Borí*, which today is practiced in the West African Savannah, especially in modern Nigeria.

There was also a pragmatic element in the behavior of West African rulers. Many were conscious that a complete rejection of local religion would have been unacceptable to the rural and agricultural populations. Consequently, these kings practiced "dual kingship"—appearing as Muslim rulers in the cities and as traditional rulers in rural settings. This practice is evident in the epic oral account of Sundiata, the heroic founder of the empire of Ancient Mali. In battle he appears as the "hunter king," but in the cities he dresses "in the robes of a Muslim king."

Finally, the extensive trade into and out of the savannahs also meant that this region exerted a cultural influence on the regions with which it traded. *Borí*, for example, spread into North Africa, likely in part via the influence of enslaved women. Further, traders from the savannah states became an important conduit for spreading Islam into other parts of West Africa. Traders from Songhai were frequently identified as *Wangara*, a term often misidentified as an ethnicity rather than as an economic designation (a fine example of the intersection of trade and culture). The Wangara dominated not only trade within the Songhai empire, but also trade to the forest regions of the south, where they exchanged salt, copper, manufactured goods, and slaves for not only gold, but also caffeine-rich kola nuts, which were becoming a popular commodity in the savannahs. To the east, trade along the Savannah also seems to have been a critical component in the introduction of Islam to the Hausa city states of northern Nigeria. A passage from the *Kano Chronicle*, a written history of the important trading city of Kano, describes economic exchange with the west in the fifteenth century:

> The whole of the products of the West were brought to Hausaland [and] roads from Bornu to Gwanja [were opened]. In [King] Yakabu's time [1452–1463] the Fulani came to Hausaland from Melle, bringing with them books on Divinity and Etymology . . . At this time, too, the [Berber Tuaregs] came to Gobir, and salt became common in Hausaland.

As the Songhai Empire went into decline and was eventually overthrown by a Moroccan invasion in 1591, many Islamic traders left the region to seek their fortunes elsewhere in West Africa. Often referred to as the "*Dyula* Diaspora" (*Dyula* being another common term for "trader") this dispersal of Muslim traders throughout the region was yet another factor in the spread of Islam in West Africa.

New Sources of Salt

The decline of the savannah empires did not bring end the salt trade in West Africa, although it saw a significant alteration in the nature of that trade, as the trade changed due to a new source of salt from centers of production that developed in the central Sudan, particularly in the region around Lake Chad.

Probably around the sixteenth century, salt production began to expand in the region around Lake Chad—then under the control of the powerful state of Kanem-Borno. The last of the string of lakes that once extended along the southern fringe of the Sahara, Lake Chad and many small (often seasonal) lakes in the region were excellent locations for the collection of a great variety of salts, which could be gathered from exposed lakebeds or shorelines during the dry season. Indeed, the chemical complexity of these salts was recognized by the local populations, who had specific names for different varieties. Salts high in sodium chloride were used exclusively as seasoning for food. The most valuable variety was called *beza*, which was sold in relatively small quantities tied up in leather bags. Other recognized types were *baboul*, *manda*, and *mangul*. The different flavors of these salts meant that recipes called for specific kinds of salt. Another category of salts, those containing significant components of sodium carbonate and sodium sulphate, are generally called *natrons*. Some of the natrons were used as lower-cost salt alternatives, others were used as medicines (sodium carbonates were popular treatments for stomach ailments—just as today sodium carbonate is an active ingredient in Alka Seltzer), and some as a dietary supplements for livestock.

Some varieties of natron are quite poisonous, but they were still useful and valuable. One, known as *gwangwarasa*, is a very pure sodium sulfate, and was in high demand in the region of the Hausa States to facilitate the tanning of leather, which was a rapidly growing industry at the time. *Farinkanwa*, another caustic natron, was used in the making of soap, glass, ink, and to help break down indigo into a soluble form for dye works.

The processing of salt and natron in the Lake Chad region was not as easy as simply collecting them from the lakebeds (Map 2.2). Most

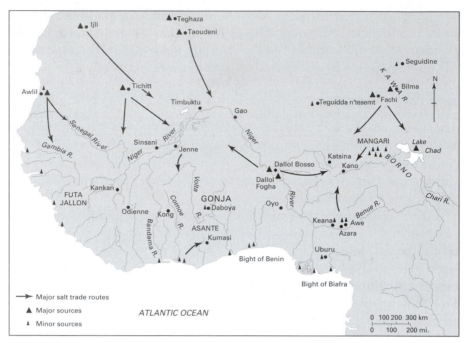

MAP 2.2   Sources of salt and natron in the western and central Sudan.

varieties of salts, particularly the higher value edible and industrial salts, demanded a degree of processing to purify and refine them. For edible salts, processing was undertaken via the use of large solar-heated evaporation pits, as much as three meters deep and six meters square. Flow into the pits was regulated from larger dam-controlled pools. If the salinity of the pits was properly managed, salt crystals would form on the surface and could be skimmed off. The salt was then packed into cone-shaped molds for drying. The resulting cones of salt weighed around 15 kilograms each, and were ready for wholesale export. Once they reached their destination, they could be cut cross-wise into disks of varying sizes to be sold to local buyers. Other salts demanded even more processing. *Manda* and *baboul* had to be filtered, placed in small pots, and then boiled in furnaces to produce the final product. One estimate is that salt production in the central Sudan peaked at around 15,000 metric tons per year—perhaps double the amount of salt being transported to the savannahs from sources in the northwestern Sahara. Thus, it is clear that far from relying on transport from afar, by the seventeenth and early eighteenth centuries, West Africans were producing rather than importing the bulk of their salt.

It appears, however, that local demand for salt still outstretched supply by as much as 50,000 metric tons a year, highlighting the ongoing salt-poor status of West Africa. Nonetheless, markets for salts and natrons from the central Sudan were far-flung and, apparently growing. Not only were the Hausa city-states a major source of demand, but the growing Asante state in the region of modern Ghana was also a market for salts from Kanem-Borno. Interestingly, the growing popularity of tobacco imported from the Americas seems to have greatly expanded the demand for salt. Rather than smoking, most Africans of the period preferred to take tobacco in the form of snuff, which is inhaled through the nose. Different varieties of salt and natron, added to the snuff, were considered to greatly improve the quality of the experience.

The ongoing demand for and growing value of the salt trade did not escape the attention of states in the region. Kanem-Borno, by virtue of benefit of location, controlled much of the process of production and trade. During the seventeenth century, Kanem-Borno's expansion north-ward (at the expense of the desert-dwelling Tuareg) was likely moti-vated by the desire to gain control of the valuable salt deposits north of the Komodugu River. Evidence suggests that the Kanem-Borno, rather than closely regulating the salt trade through a formal bureaucracy, doled out the rights to exploit salt deposits and trade salt as a form of political patronage—a characteristic of the fairly decentralized nature of African states at the time. Kanem-Borno retained dominance until a major drought hit the region in the early eighteenth century, which allowed the Tuareg, who were less dependent on agricultural output, to again gain control over the northern salt-producing regions. The uni-fication of the Hausa city-states in the form of the Sokoto Caliphate in the early nineteenth century, also resulted in Kanem-Borno's loss of salt-producing regions along its western borders. In general, however, the nineteenth century saw a decline in the production of West African salt, as the growing importation of increasingly cheap and highly refined European salt began to undercut local salt production.

CONCLUSIONS: SALT AND CULTURE IN CHINA AND WEST AFRICA

Salt clearly played a central role in the economic, political, and cul-tural development of China and West Africa, but did so in strikingly different ways. In both regions, demand for this necessary dietary element kept pace with the growth of sedentary agricultural and urban societies. In both regions, salt also was a crucial component in the rise of state power. Similarly, the development of culture was in no small way tied to the trade in salt.

However, there are also striking differences. China's more substantial and varied salt resources meant that salt was acquired primarily through internal production, rather than importation. Similarly, the highly centralized and bureaucratic structure of Chinese government meant that control over salt, along with iron, became a central aspect of political culture in the region. More so, control over salt was a key means by which the state involved itself in the lives of even the most remote elements of the population from a very early date. Thus, control over internal salt production and trade was a means by which Chinese culture was created and reinforced because it linked rulers and the ruled across space and social class. Further, because control over salt was of far greater fiscal importance to the Chinese government than exports, such as silk or porcelain, the state was encouraged to be inward rather than outward looking. Quite to the contrary, the importation of salt from distant regions of the Sahara meant that the early wealth of West African states such as Ghana, Mali, and Songhai was based not simply on production, but also trade. As trading states, these societies were constantly influencing and being influenced by their foreign trading partners. In particular, the trade in salt, along with gold, was a major conduit for the introduction of Islam first into the West African savannahs and eventually the forests. Thus, in West Africa, salt fostered the gradual inclusion of West Africans, particularly political and economic elites, into the global culture of the *Dar al-Islam*. Even as production of salts expanded in the central Sudan during the sixteenth and later centuries, long-distance trade and a more *laissez-faire* approach to government involvement continued to define the West African approach experience with salt.

SOURCES

China

A Debate over the Salt Monopoly
Huan Kuan, *Discourses on Salt and Iron.*

The Discourses is a remarkable historical document, set down sometime between 74 and 49 B.C.E. by the Confucian scholar Huan Kuan. It is a somewhat formalized account of a debate called by Emperor Zhao around 81 B.C.E.. As already noted, the goal was to have scholars examine the advantages and disadvantages of continuing the government's control over two of the Chinese economy's most important commodities: salt and iron. In general, the "Lord Grand Secretary" represents a pro-monopoly position associated with the Legalist tradition. The "Literati" represent the anti-monopoly perspective favored by Confucians. What follows is a tiny excerpt from a debate that totals 60 chapters.

Ask yourself the following questions. Why does the Lord Grand Secretary see the monopolies as beneficial? Why do the Literati see them as harmful? What do your answers suggest about these two schools of philosophy? Both the Literati and the Lord Grand Secretary compare the Chinese economy to a patient and the government to a physician. What does this metaphor say about the ancient Chineses' political and economic sophistication? Do you see anything familiar in the arguments presented? If so, what? What is unfamiliar? What conclusions follow from these last two answers?

CHAPTER XIV: THE RATIO OF PRODUCTION

The Lord Grand Secretary: The principle of governing a country consists in removing the noxious and hoeing out the unruly. Only then will the people enjoy equal treatment, and find satisfaction under their own roofs. His Excellency has busied himself with statistical calculations to increase the state revenue. The resources of salt and iron are monopolized in order to put down the rich traders and big merchants. Consequently, in spite of the fact that our armies made expeditions east and west, expenditures were well provided for without increasing the levies and taxes.

The Literati: The inferior physician does not know the lines of artery and vein, or the difference between the blood and vital fluid.

He stabs in his needle blindly without any effect on the disease,[1] and only injures the skin and flesh. Now [the Government] desires to subtract from the superabundant to add to the needy. And yet the rich grow richer, and the poor grow poorer. Severe laws and penalties are intended to curb the tyrannical and suppress malefactors. Yet the wicked still persist.

The Secretary: But when His Excellency, the Minister, in his capacity of Grain Intendant, took over the administration of the Imperial treasury, with his "needle pricks" and "cauterizing" he stimulated the stagnant flow of wealth, and opened up the pulsing sources of profit along the hundred arteries. As a result all commodities were circulated, and the Government got substantial revenue. At that time, expeditions were sent in four directions against the rebellious and disorderly. The expenses for chariots[2] and armor, and the rewards for conquests and captives, were estimated by billions. All, however, was supplied by the treasury. This is certainly . . . the boon of the salt and iron monopoly.

Salt Production in Fourteenth-century China
Chen Chun, *Aobo Tu.*

The Aobo Tu is an unusually detailed account of the process of salt manufacture in coastal China during the Yuan Dynasty (1279–1368). The original document included not only the sections of poetry excerpted below, but also more formal prose descriptions and illustrations. Comprising 47 chapters, these perspectives provide a remarkable understanding of both the science and art of Chinese salt production in the thirteenth and fourteenth centuries.
    Consider the following. What is the narrator's attitude towards the manufacture of salt? Towards the laborers who produce it? What sort of technologies are required to produce salt in this fashion? How does the narrator seem to understand the relationship between humanity and nature? What general conclusions follow from your answers to these questions?

10. Diverting the Tidewater by Opening a New Channel Farther into the Sea
Somebody said that with a single hand a river can be blocked up,
but what I have seen is that with the strength of a multitude the sea
    can be conducted.

The Southeast is a great store of revenue and wealth,
the source bringing forth goods and wealth is without exhaustion.
Ten thousand *qing* of the sea's waves, they can be taken without
 restriction.
The hurrying spades of one thousand workers are arriving like the
 wind.
After a little while, the sea is guided to enter the plain.
If this is not by human power, it just would be the achievement of
 heaven.

18. Paring the Earth and Leveling It
Damp mud does not withstand pounding,
and small weeds do not withstand digging.
In all four directions, evenness and cleanliness is valued,
and everywhere one has to guard against leaking cracks.
Between the buffaloes, stone rollers are placed,
thus erasing the traces of deer which have passed by.
Before long, boiling has to start;
salt matters cannot be delayed.

23. Collecting the Ashes by Paring and Sweeping
Sweeping to and fro, a thousand brooms are being worn down;
pushing and pulling, the elbows are moving forward and
 backward.
A hundred heaps, a thousand heaps, people are hurrying here and there.
By tasting and tasting again, the mouths of the people get salty.
A thousand workers are entering the spreading place contending for the
 exposure of the ashes.
Both skilled and unskilled hands expose the ashes.
All you workers have to be careful and should not sigh about
 your pains,
because this days work is the basis of forming the salt the next day.

46. The Loose Salt is Collected Daily
How much is boiled in one day,
and how much is collected daily?
One is only afraid that the quota cannot be reached,
thus not only meeting with the superiors sneering and scolding but
 also with beating.

The daily levies have their working schedule,
and for official affairs no wasting of time is allowed.
Month after month, no false reports are presented,
and one does not dare to cause delays to the salt supervising officials.

West Africa—On the Road to Ghana
Abu Ubaydallah al-Bakri, *The Book of Roads and Provinces*

Al-Bakri was one of the greatest scholars of the mid- to late eleventh century. A resident of Cordoba in Islamic Spain (al-Andalus), he wrote extensively on history, science, and politics, though he is perhaps best known for his geographical text, The Book of Roads and Provinces. The selection below is a short excerpt from this work, describing the Saharan and Savannah regions of West Africa.

Ask yourself about al-Bakri's audience and sources. What sort of information was al-Bakri's audience apparently looking for? From where do you think al-Bakri received his information? What conclusions are suggested by your answers? Ask also, how difficult does the trek to the salt mines appear to have been? Finally, what perspective does al-Balri seem to have of the inhabitants of Ancient Ghana, and what do you conclude from your answer?

There are five stages from Wadi[3] Dar'a to the Wadi Tarja, where the desert begins. There you travel over the desert plain, finding water every two or three days, until you come to the beginning of the arid waste at the well called Tazamt. It contains spring water which is not sweet, but rather salty, and which was made to issue from very hard rock . . . To the east from there is a well called Bir al-Jammanlin, near which is another well called Nalil. None of these contain sweet water. Between these three wells and the lands of Islam there is four days traveling. From there one goes the same distance to the mountains called in the Berber language Adrar an Wuzzal, which means "Mountains of Iron." From these mountains the waste extends for eight days before one attains water . . . From the aforementioned wells, one enters a wasteland where water is found at a distance of four days, and then one reaches Izal, which is a mountain in the desert.

Among the remarkable things found in the desert is the salt-mine which is at a distance of two days marching from the Great Waste and twenty days from Sijilmasa.[4] The salt is uncovered by removing a layer of earth as other minerals and precious stones are dug up. The salt is found two fathoms[5] or less below the surface and is cut [in blocks] as stone is cut. This mine is called Tatantal. Above the mine stands a castle built from rock-salt. The houses, battlements, and rooms are all of this salt. From this mine, salt is transported to Sijilmasa, Ghana, and other countries of the land of the Sudan.[6] Work there continues uninterruptedly and merchants arrive in a constant stream for it has an enormous production.

There is another salt mine in the land of the Banu Gudala at a place called Awlil on the coast. From there too caravans carry salt to the neighboring countries.

Ghana and the customs of its inhabitants
Ghana is the title given to their kings; the name of the region is Awkar, and their king today, namely in the year 460/1067/68[7] is Tunka Manin. . . . The name of his predecessor was Basi and he became their ruler at the age of 85. He led a praisworthy life on account of his love of justice and friendship for the Muslims . . . Basi was maternal uncle of Tunka Manin. . . . This Tunka Manin is powerful, rules an enormous kingdom, and possesses great authority. . . .

On every donkey-load of salt when it is brought into the country their king levies one golden dinar,[8] and two dinars when it is sent out. From a load of copper, the king's due is five mithqals, and from a load of other goods ten mithqals. The best gold found in his land comes from the town of Ghiyaru, which is eighteen days traveling distant from the king's town over a country inhabited by tribes of the Sudan whose dwellings are continuous.

The Salt Economy of Fourteenth-century West Africa
Abu Abdallah Mohammed Ibn Battuta, *A Donation to Those Interested in Curiosities*

Ibn Battuta (1304–1369) was perhaps the greatest traveler of the premodern world. Born in Morocco, he traveled extensively in Africa, the Middle East, India, Central and Southeast Asia, and possibly southern China. More so, Ibn Battuta was a keen observer who narrated his experiences in remarkable detail. The following excerpt comes from his last adventure, a journey taken in 1352–1354, which took him across the Sahara and to the states of the West African Savannah, most notably Mali, which lay 1,500 miles south of Morocco.

This excerpt, part of a much longer description of the lands and peoples of West Africa, allows the reader to glean quite a bit of insight into the role that salt played in the lives and economies of West Africa in the fourteenth century. Exactly what were those roles? Be as specific as possible.

I set off at the beginning of God's month of Muharram in the year 753/1352 with a caravan whose leader was Abu Muhammad Yandakan al-Musufi, may God have mercy on him. In the caravan was a company of merchants of Sijilmasa and others. After 25 days we arrived at Taghaza. This is a village with nothing good about it. One of its marvels is that its houses and mosque are of rock salt and its roofs of camel skins. It has no trees, but is nothing but sand with a salt mine. They dig in the earth for the salt, which is found in great slabs lying one upon the other as though they have been shaped and placed underground. A camel carries two slabs of it. Nobody lives there except the slaves of the Masufa[9] who dig for the salt. They live on the dates imported to them from Dar'a and Sijilmasa, on camel-meat, and on *anili*[10] imported from the land of the Sudan. The Sudan come to them from their land and carry the salt away. One load of it is sold at Iwalatan for eight or ten mithqals, and at the city of Mali for twenty or thirty mithqals. It has sometimes fetched 40 mithqals.

The Sudan use salt for currency as gold and silver is used. They cut it into pieces and use it for their transactions. Despite the meanness of the village of Taghaza they deal with *qintar* upon *qintar*[11] of gold there.

The traveler [in the Sudan] does not carry any supplies, [whether staple food] or condiment nor any money, but carries only pieces of salt and the glass trinkets which people call *nazm* and a few spicy condiments. What pleases them most is cloves, mastic, and *tasarghant*, which is their incense. When he reaches a village, the women of the Sudan bring *anili* and milk and chickens and flour and rice and *funi* (which is like mustard seed and kuskusu and *asida* are made from it) and cowpea bean and he buys from them what he wants.

NOTES

1. A reference to acupuncture.
2. A traditional description of war materials. Chinese armies no longer used chariots.
3. A wadi is a desert depression. Here it probably means an oasis.

4. A Saharan trading center in southern Morocco.
5. Twelve feet.
6. "The Blacks."
7. A.H. (in the year of the Hijra) 460, according to the Islamic lunar calendar; 1067–68 C.E. according to the Western solar calendar. The Islamic calendar begins with Muhammad's hijra, or departure, from Mecca for Medina; the Western calendar begins with the putative birth year of Jesus.
8. A standard gold coin in the Islamic World that weighed 4.72 grams, or one mithqal (see Chapter 2, note 24).
9. A Berber people of the western Sahara.
10. Millet.
11. "Weight upon weight." In other words, a large amount.

Sugar and Slavery

SUGAR CANE AND SWEET FOODS

Most mammals like the taste of sweet foods. Humans are no exception. But some regions of the world have made sweet foods a bigger part of their diet than others. In some cases this can be attributed to environment. People who live in the Arctic and eat few plant foods are not destined to eat many sweets. But even in the tropics, where plant sugars are easy to get, some cultures place a greater emphasis on sweet foods than others. In Europe, once sugar became available, the English came to consume more of it than the Italians or Spaniards. So one of the questions we need to consider here is why some people consume so much sugar and others so little. The other question worth thinking about is why one plant source of sugar came to so totally dominate the world's sugar trade.

Some cuisines have embraced sweet foods. India, the Arab world, and Western Europe were the biggest consumers of sugar during the time period that concerns us (Map 3.1). By contrast, Southeast Asian cooking makes less use of sugar, and sweets are less a part of people's diets. This is despite the fact that Southeast Asia's environment is well-suited to growing sugar cane, much better suited in fact than Europe, where far more sugar was consumed. So environment does not entirely explain the differences in people's consumption of sugar. Sidney Mintz has argued that some people eat larger amounts of sugar than others because macroeconomic and social forces push them in that direction. He sees a strong link between the emerging industrial working class in Britain and the rise in sugar consumption. His explanation works nicely for Europe, but it is harder to make it fit with India or the Arab world. Why some people consume so much sugar and others so much less remains an unresolved question.

Processed sugar may have been an exotic novelty in medieval Europe, but it is quite ancient in South Asia. Long before Europeans encountered sugar, Indians were using it in a number of different forms. India produces a staggering variety of sugars and sweet foods. Just as we in the West have learned to think of salt as a single product rather than something that comes in many forms and varieties, so too have we learned to think of sugar as a single substance that comes in white, brown, and confectioner's varieties. In India, sugars are produced from many different plant sources and these often have unique culinary uses. *Jaggery*, which is made from palm sap, and *gur*, which refers to syrups made from a number of different plant sources, are the names given to these sugars. Sugar can also be made from date syrup or even ground dates. Any of these sugars would have a much more complex taste than plain white sugar and each is often preferred for particular dishes. Even Europeans, who initially had many fewer sweeteners, had honey, the flavor of which is also highly variable. So there are many ways, often culturally determined, of sweetening food.

The dominance of sugar cane is easier to explain than the question of why some cultures consume more processed sugar than others. The plant, a member of the grass family, grows nine or ten feet in height, and its thick stem is full of juice that is rich in sucrose. Like other grasses, it grows back when cut, so once in production cane fields do not need to be replanted. Under modern conditions, a single acre of sugar cane produces 5.6 tons of sugar and 1.35 tons of molasses. That is roughly eight million calories of food. To produce a comparable number of calories would require

MAP 3.1   Sugar producing regions of the Atlantic and Mediterranean Seas.

nine to twelve acres of wheat. Sugar cane outperforms any other plant when it comes to calories per unit of land.

To coax that bounty from the cane requires labor—lots of labor. Before mechanization became a factor, sugar cane required one worker per acre. These high-labor requirements are the result of the plant's finicky nature. Even in the tropics, sugar cane only reaches its full yield when irrigated. So plantation workers had to create and then manage irrigation systems to keep the crop wet. But the biggest labor demands came during the harvest. Sugar cane juice is rich in sugar when it is harvested, but the amount of sugar in the sap begins to decline as soon as the cane is harvested. So there can be no delay between harvest and moving the cane to the place where it will be processed. And processing is a matter of great urgency lest sugar content drop while cane waits to be processed. As a result sugar cane processing has always taken place close to the point of production and usually on the plantation itself. Thus, at the center of each plantation or cluster of plantations was a mill. In the mill was equipment for crushing the cane and extracting the juice, a boiling house where the juice was cooked down, and storage sheds where the sugar was separated from the molasses and formed into loaves. The final step of refining the sugar was done, if it was done at all, elsewhere (Figure 3.1).

FIGURE 3.1 An eighteenth century image of a sugar-boiling house shows workers using perforated paddles to skim debris from sugar cane juice while it is being reduced by boiling.

Source: University of Bristol, Information Services.

Sugar is refined by removing the molasses that both flavors and colors less refined sugars. This is now done with centrifuges that force the molasses out of the sugar. In earlier times, various degrees of refining were done by rinsing the sugar repeatedly with small amounts of water. The rinsed sugar was placed in inverted conical forms and allowed to sit for months while the molasses sank to the bottom. The result was a solid loaf of sugar that had some portions that were nearly white and others that were darker. Many mountains in New England are named for their resemblance to these loaves. What we now call brown sugar is refined sugar into which molasses has been mixed. The sugars produced by the early sugar industry were probably browner than modern white sugars, but without the moisture of brown sugar.

During the harvest these mills usually ran around the clock to ensure that there was no delay in processing the cane. And the conditions in the mills were hellish. The crushing equipment could crush human limbs as easily as it crushed cane. Axes were kept handy to sever crushed arms. The boiling houses were hot and as the juice thickened it became viscous, sticky, and the source of dangerous burns. The danger to the workers was exacerbated by the long hours they put in during the harvest. This combination of high labor needs and terrible working conditions meant that it was hard to find people seeking careers in the sugar industry. So, wherever sugar has been grown it has been associated with involuntary labor.

THE ORIGINS OF THE PLANTATION COMPLEX

Sugar cane is native to Southeast Asia and was probably domesticated thousands of years ago in New Guinea. It spread from there to India, where it became one of several sources of sugar. Cane sugar seems to have been virtually unknown in the ancient Mediterranean. The Romans made extensive use of honey in their cooking and to sweeten wine. There are a few references in Roman geographical literature to the existence in India of canes that produce a sweet sap, and it is a bit curious that, despite the widespread Roman trade with India, no sugar came to the Mediterranean as part of a shipment of spice, but perhaps the perishable and soluble nature of sugar militated against it in a seaborne trade.

It was not until the rise of Islam and the Arab conquests of the Sind (modern Pakistan) that sugar was introduced into the Mediterranean world. The Arabs developed a passion for sugar that nearly rivaled that of the Indians, and eventually introduced sugar cane into the wetter parts of the Middle East, including the Eastern Mediterranean. Sugar production also spread into parts of Muslim North Africa, southern Spain and into the islands of Sicily and Sardinia. Almost certainly some of this sugar ended up in the hands of the emerging merchant class and the nobility, but it was not until the crusades that elite Europeans became regular consumers of sugar, and it was in the context of the crusades that they learned to grow it.

The First Crusade (1096–1102) captured Jerusalem in 1099 and, along with it, a good portion of the rest of the Holy Land. The victorious crusaders then carved the captured land into feudal principalities, several of which enjoyed a precarious existence down to the end of the thirteenth century. For almost two hundred years these crusader states attracted numerous additional crusaders, who came to defend the lands against Islamic counter attacks, and colonists from every level of European society. Inevitably, these new arrivals learned new ways and habits while living as a ruling minority among a majority population of Eastern Christians and Muslims. Of course, there were tensions on both sides, but there are accounts, some written by Arabs, that indicate that some Western colonists, or Franks, as they were called, began to dress and eat more like Arabs and Turks. Usamah ibn Munqidh, a twelfth-century Syrian, describes how one of his men was invited to a Frank's home for a meal. He came, but ate nothing fearing that his host might serve him foods that are forbidden to Muslims. His host noticed his reluctance, and told him that he had hired an Egyptian cook and no pork was served in his house. In addition to adopting Muslim dietary practices, the settlers also got into the habit of eating sugar and spices. Overtime, they also began to grow sugar (or at least control lands that produced sugar) and to export it to their homelands. In 1291 the Franks were driven from their last foothold on the mainland of Syria-Palestine but were still entrenched in Greece and on many Eastern Mediterranean islands, including Cyprus, which they held from 1191 to 1571. According to Phillip Curtin, it was on Cyprus that most of the basic features of the plantation complex that would eventually spread to the Americas coalesced.

The key players in this process were Italian merchants, who began to invest in sugar production in Cyprus and other parts of the Mediterranean. To make their estates pay off, they poured funds into extensive irrigation systems and the latest in milling technology, and set out to get as reliable and manageable a labor force as they could find (Figure 3.2). For this they turned to slave labor. Slave labor had long been part of the Arab sugar industry, and the crusades had kept both Muslim and Christian growers supplied with war captives. But as the crusades petered out, Italian sugar producers turned to new sources for slaves, especially the slave markets of the Black Sea. This approach to sugar production—with heavy investment in irrigation, machinery, and imported slaves—spread through the Frankish-controlled regions of the Mediterranean, accompanied by Italian capital and expertise.

By the late fifteenth century, there was a standard way of growing sugar. It was grown on plantations, the plantations included a small factory that processed the cane into sugar, and the work was done by slaves. This growing supply of sugar was consumed mostly by the European elite, who used it in ways that may seem unfamiliar to us. Often sugar was treated as a spice or as a drug. It appears in lists of spices and was often used to flavor savory dishes and meats, much the way we might now add salt to dishes to enhance other flavors. A modern survival of this is our taste for sugar- or honey-glazed ham. Sugar was also considered to have medicinal uses. Because refined white sugar looked so pure, it was thought to have a variety of positive effects on peoples' health. For a while it was even touted as an excellent dentifrice. One can only imagine the effect of daily brushing with a teaspoon of sugar.

Sugar was also used to demonstrate the wealth and status of the European elites who were able to serve it to guests. This might take several forms. Sugar was served on silver plates that also held other spices for guests to either eat directly or add to their food. It was also combined with spice to make spicy sweets called "subtleties," which were eaten at the table of the rich and powerful. Eating subtleties was a way of ostentatiously consuming wealth. Their symbolic role was sometimes emphasized by wrapping edible silver or gold foil around them. Sugar was also used to create elaborate edible sculptures for use at banquets. No other food is so easily shaped as sugar. The structural possibilities in sugar sculpture were near endless. What is interesting about this is how sugar consumption fit the economic and social patterns of the time. In an aristocratic society, sugar was used to demonstrate the social worth of those who consumed it. It was not a major source of calories, even for the elite.

In the fifteenth century, a number of new developments began to push sugar production into new places and to change the nature of

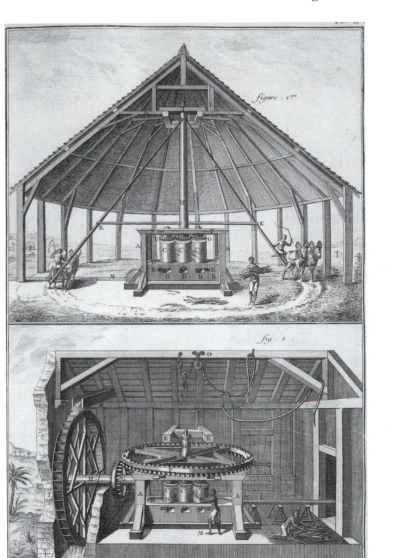

OEconomie Rustique,
Sucrerie.

FIGURE 3.2 This image shows two versions of eighteenth century roller mills. One uses animal power, the other water. The presence of these mills in the midst of the sugar plantations made the sugar trade almost as industrial as it was agricultural.

Source: University of Virginia Library.

sugar consumption in Europe. In the early part of the fifteenth century the Portuguese began to explore the Atlantic coast of Africa. In the process of doing this they rediscovered the Canary Islands and discovered Madeira. The Canaries were inhabited by a people called the Guanches; Madeira was uninhabited. It soon dawned in on the Portuguese that Madeira was well-suited to sugar production. In 1455, sugar was introduced to Madeira by the Portuguese who imported slaves, mostly Guanches from the Canaries. Toward the end of the fifteenth century, Madeira was the single biggest sugar supplier to Europe; by 1480 the Belgian port of Antwerp was sending 70 ships a year to Madeira, and in 1493, Madeira produced 760 metric tons of sugar. The island also represented a new type of economic entity. Its sugar had to be transported over long distances to reach its market in Europe, and labor, manufactured goods, capital, and expertise were all imported. Madeira was as economically specialized as a place could be in the fifteenth century.

The other crucial change that occurred in the middle of the fifteenth century was a shift in the source of slaves. In 1453 the Ottoman Turks finally captured Constantinople. With the Byzantine capital, which sits astride the Bosporus, in their hands they were able to prevent the Italians from entering the Black Sea. As a result, the main source of slaves for the Mediterranean slave trade was lost. At almost exactly the same time, the Portuguese began to buy slaves on the West African coast, and Lisbon became the leading slave market in Europe. As the Guanche population of the Canaries died off from disease, warfare, and the effects of slave raiding, enslaved Africans became increasingly associated with sugar production and with the institution of slavery.

That link was further strengthened on the island of Sao Tome. Sao Tome, which is almost exactly on the equator, lies off the coast of the modern Central African country known as Gabon. Sao Tome was colonized by the Portuguese in 1490. It was wet and warm, and sugar cane did well there. The Portuguese, however, did not. Madeira and the Canaries were fairly hospitable to European settlement, thus much of the sugar there was produced by free Portuguese settlers. Sao Tome was much more tropical, so diseases like malaria and yellow fever, another deadly mosquito borne disease, caused Portuguese settlers to die at an appalling rate. In the early sixteenth century there were only 50 Portuguese there, and these were mostly exiled convicts and converts from Judaism. So lethal was the climate that the Portuguese used it as a form of de facto capital punishment for priests, whom church law protected from the death penalty. Priests they wished to get rid of were given a parish in Sao Tome, with the expectation that they would perish soon after. Thus, the use of free settlers to grow sugar cane was out of the question in Sao Tome and other sources of labor were needed.

The labor problem was resolved by the use of African slaves in all stages of production. Sao Tome was near the Kingdom of Kongo, an African state allied with Portugal. Kongo had a vigorous foreign policy that resulted in the presence of large numbers of war captives. The kings of Kongo were able to strengthen their relationship with the Portuguese, and rid themselves of potentially dangerous war captives, by selling them to the Portuguese as slaves. The Portuguese exchanged some of these slaves for gold in West Africa, they took some to Lisbon to be sold in the European slave market, and they moved some to Sao Tome to serve the sugar industry there.

On Madeira and in the Canaries, the workforce included Africans, Europeans, Guanches, and Arabs. It also included many free laborers who worked alongside the slaves. In Sao Tome, virtually the entire workforce was African and enslaved. There were some Italian technical experts there along with Portuguese landowners and a few forlorn priests, but otherwise Sao Tome was African. Sao Tome was also much farther from its European markets than Madeira. Nonetheless, it was briefly a major force in the sugar trade, producing as much sugar as Madeira by the middle of the sixteenth century.

Sao Tome went into decline in the second half of the sixteenth century for several reasons. The first was competition from the New World, especially Brazil which began to produce sugar in a serious way in the second half of the sixteenth century. The second was a common side effect of the use of slave labor–slave revolts. Given the high mortality rates for recently arrived Europeans in Sao Tome, the Portuguese could only provide the most limited sort of security. One of the major aspects of a slave-based plantation system is violence. Plantation owners need to use violence or the threat of violence to keep their slaves disciplined and at work. In Sao Tome the weakness of the Portuguese administration combined with the rugged mountainous interior of the island made it easy for escaped slaves to hide. Escaped slaves withdrew into the interior from where they conducted raids on the coastal plantations. The volcanic peaks of the interior gave sufficient refuge that they were able to maintain their rebellion into the nineteenth century. The costs they inflicted on the plantations were not the only cause of Sao Tome's decline, but they were a significant factor.

Sao Tome and the other Atlantic islands were a proving ground for sugar production in the Americas. First, the Portuguese experience in the Atlantic demonstrated that sugar could profitably be transported over long distances. When Sao Tome first began to produce sugar it was the most distant outpost of European production on the planet. Silk and spices might have come to Europe from farther afield, but nowhere else on the planet was a colony producing something entirely for so distant a market. It was also the place where the link between African slavery and sugar production was forged, a link that would remain virtually unbroken for the next 400 years. Sao Tome may now be an obscure and impoverished place, but it was once on the leading edge of a commercial revolution.

SUGAR IN THE NEW WORLD

The European discovery of the Americas marks one of the major watersheds in world history. The economic, political, demographic, and biological significance of the event is hard to overstate. The introduction of sugar production into the Americas was only one of the many consequences of the Columbian Exchange, but it was an exceedingly significant one.

The potential of these islands to produce sugar was almost immediately apparent. Columbus' description of Hispaniola in his initial report of 1493 made reference to the presence of mastic, a gum that comes from the islands of the eastern Mediterranean. There is no mastic on Hispaniola, but Columbus seems to have mentally put the island into a category that would include other sugar-producing islands. By 1513 there was a sugar mill on Hispaniola, though at first sugar production was low and overshadowed by attempts at ranching and mining.

Hispaniola is, of course, ideal sugar country, and in the eighteenth and nineteenth centuries it would become a major sugar producer. What initially limited early sugar production there was a shortage of labor. The most obvious answer to the question of who should do the work on the sugar plantations was the local Indians—Arawak speakers called Tainos. But the Tainos, whose world had been totally turned upside down by the arrival of Spanish colonists, died at rate that astonished the Spaniards. The Spaniards, or possibly their animals, had introduced hitherto unknown diseases in the

Caribbean. Those diseases took a tremendous toll on the Tainos, who also seem to have lost the will to resist the destruction of their culture and very identity. The Tainos were at the forefront of a massive die off of native Americans, a process that would claim possibly as much as 90 percent of the populations of Mesoamerica and the Caribbean in the first century after the initial contact.[1] Perhaps because they were the first to experience the trauma, both physiological and psychological, of contact with Europeans, they succumbed more thoroughly than most other groups of Indians. As was the case with the Guanches, the Tainos are no more.

Even though they imported Indians from other areas of the Americas to Hispaniola, the Spaniards could not create a self-sustaining slave population. So, as a labor source, Indians were at best a short-term solution. The other possibility, again following previous Atlantic models, was to use the labor of European settlers. On Madeira and the Canaries this had worked well. The difference, which made European labor work poorly, seems to have been the abundant opportunities in the Americas. People who had come all the way to the Caribbean, did not do so to do the backbreaking work that sugar cane demanded of those called to its service. Even those who crossed the Atlantic under duress soon found they had better options, such as serving as mercenary soldiers, than toiling in the cane fields. Entrepreneurs were also initially not enthusiastic about producing sugar in the New World. Why plow capital and labor into an enterprise that might take years to pay off when there seemed to be far easier and quicker ways of tapping the seemingly inexhaustible riches of the Americas?

The first major effort to profit from sugar production in the American colonies only began in the second half of the sixteenth century in Brazil, a region that initially had been of little interest to the Portuguese, who used it primarily as a source for logwood, a valuable hardwood that is also a dyestuff. This limited Brazil trade did not appeal to the Portuguese nobility, who sought more glamorous opportunity in Asia, but it attracted the attention of Portuguese merchants and even a few from outside of Portugal. That outsiders were dabbling in the Brazil trade, however minor, eventually came to the notice of the Portuguese state, and it took action to consolidate its control over the Brazilian coast. To do this, the Portuguese divided the coast into strips, each with a certain amount of coastline and extending indefinitely into the interior. Each of these was granted as a feudal fief to a "captain," who was essentially sovereign in his fief. Apparently this was an attempt to use Mediterranean models of colonization in the New World and an example of the continuity of Portuguese efforts at colonization in the Mediterranean, the Atlantic Islands, and the New World.

These feudal land grants soon failed economically and reverted to the crown. But they had drawn merchants and other non-noble Portuguese to Brazil and it was these people who noticed Brazil's potential for sugar production. The center of Brazil's sugar production was the area called Bahia ("bay" in Portuguese) which surrounds the city of Salvador. It is about 12 degrees south of the equator, and contains about 4,000 square miles of ideal sugar ground. As such, it was much larger than any of its potential rivals at the time, dwarfing Sao Tome and Madeira, the main sugar producers at the time. It was also reasonably close to European markets and quite close to West Africa. Bahia and Recife (which is the other major sugar region in Brazil) are on the eastern-most part of the bulge of Brazil that extends far into the Atlantic. Consequently, a ship coming from West Africa could arrive in Bahia weeks earlier than it would arrive in the Caribbean. Thus, mortality rates in the slave trade to Bahia were much lower than those in the trade to the Caribbean, a factor that would later give Brazil a competitive advantage over its future competitors in the Caribbean.

Brazilian merchants began to plant sugar in Bahia in the middle of the sixteenth century. By the end of the century Brazil was the world's leading sugar producer. Once established in the New World, the market for sugar was such that despite slightly higher costs, sugar production spread into the Caribbean in the late seventeenth century and then took off in what is called the Sugar Revolution in the eighteenth century. By 1750, the Portuguese were growing sugar in Brazil, the English were growing it in Jamaica and Barbados, the Dutch in Surinam and the Netherlands Antilles, the Spanish in Santo Domingo, while the French produced it in Saint Domingue, as they called their half of Hispaniola. Sugar islands traded hands in royal dowries and in peace treaties. Sugar had arrived.

It is worth pausing a moment to reflect on what a revolutionary development this was. In 1400 few Europeans would have consumed carbohydrates that came from any great distance. There was a small trade in grains in Europe, but the transportation costs of grain was so high that most people got the bulk of their sustenance from grain grown within a few days' walk of where they lived; indeed, most grew their own grain.

The opening of Brazil and other tropical American regions to sugar production caused a significant increase in the amount of sugar available to Europeans and changed the way it was consumed. As Brazil, Barbados and other Caribbean producers entered the market, sugar increasingly entered the European diet. It was used in tea, coffee, and chocolate, all of which were introduced in the seventeenth century and became wildly popular in the eighteenth century. The combination of caffeine and sugar, previously unknown in the world, became central to the European diet and spread outward from there. Coffee, tea, and chocolate were the basis of what has been called the Hot Drinks Revolution, and all were consumed with sugar. In their homelands all three were originally drunk unsweetened (including chocolate) and even today East Asians do not sweeten their tea. Europeans, however, found them acceptable only with sugar. Thus, the growth in interest in hot stimulating drinks was linked with a growing interest in sweetness. Indeed, one might argue that caffeine and sugar are part of the texture of modern life, whether taken in the form of a mocha latte, sweet tea, the carbonated soft drink, or a cup of sweet chocolate, the potent combination of sugar and stimulant has swept all before it in the last 250 years.

All these foods—coffee, tea, chocolate, and sugar—were produced in tropical places, far from Europe. As their consumption became widespread in the eighteenth century, sugar became the first carbohydrate that could bear the cost of trans-oceanic trade. Europeans drinking a coffee in a café were enjoying an African stimulant mixed with a sweetener from the New World. They were enjoying a cross-cultural dietary experience made possible by world trade.

SLAVERY AND SUGAR

For others, the Hot Drinks Revolution was a bitter cup. An increase in sugar production went hand in hand (or manacle in manacle) with an increase in the use of slave labor (Figure 3.3). The Atlantic slave trade, which had been around since the middle of the fifteenth century, began to develop in a serious way after 1600. It reached its peak in the late eighteenth century. By the time it ended in the nineteenth century, approximately 11 million enslaved Africans had crossed the Atlantic, most to serve the needs of the sugar industry. North Americans tend to assume that the USA's southern states were central to the slave trade, but less than 5 percent of the slaves who crossed the Atlantic were destined

FIGURE 3.3   A nineteenth-century print showing slaves in the Caribbean harvesting sugar cane. It shows the labor intensiveness of sugar cane harvest and the disciplined nature of the work on plantations.
Source: Michael Holford photographs.

for North American markets. The vast majority ended up on sugar plantations in Brazil or the Caribbean. Sugar, more than any other crop or commodity in the Americas, was a ravenous consumer of slave labor.

The origins of the Atlantic slave trade are roughly contemporaneous with the sugar industry's move into the Atlantic. The same Portuguese navigators who found the Atlantic islands that nourished the sugar industry in the fifteenth century also learned that they could buy slaves on the West African coast. Initially the Portuguese attempted to raid for slaves just as they had in the Canaries. West Africans turned out to be much more formidable adversaries than the Guanches. The Guanches had neither metal nor horses and were susceptible to European diseases. West Africans by contrast had an ancient tradition of iron-making; indeed, the high quality ores available in parts of West Africa made local iron superior to Portuguese iron. Furthermore, the use of horses in warfare was common in the Senegambia region, where the Portuguese attempted their slave raids. In the Canaries the Portuguese confronted an enemy armed with stone-tipped weapons; in the Senegambia they encountered horsemen armed with iron weapons. Any advantage the Portuguese gained from their primitive firearms was more than outweighed by their small numbers. Perhaps more important was the role of disease. European diseases quickly killed off the Guanches, whose millennia of isolation left them vulnerable to Eurasia's many infectious diseases. West Africans, by contrast, were much less isolated and seem to have been part of the larger Afro-Eurasian disease pool. Undoubtedly Europeans introduced a few new diseases to West Africa, but there is no evidence of the type of mass die offs that would occur later in the New World. In fact the disease environment in West Africa posed serious challenges to Europeans. Virulent forms of malaria and yellow fever killed new arrivals but spared people who had survived childhood bouts with the diseases. Thus, most adult West Africans were less susceptible to these diseases than newly arrived Europeans. So any attempt to take slaves by force in West Africa was hampered by well-armed West Africans and a disease environment that made quick work of European soldiers. As a result, Europeans made few military inroads in West Africa until the nineteenth century when their military and medical technologies began to improve rapidly. Given the relatively equal balance of military power, any slaves the Portuguese, or later on the English, Dutch, French, Americans, Danes, Spanish or Germans hoped to obtain in West Africa, they had to buy.

The Portuguese were the pioneers of and the dominant force in the Atlantic slave trade down to the eighteenth century, but their commerce along the West African coast involved much more than slaves. There they, and later other Europeans, bought ivory, malagueta pepper, hides, and above all gold. In fact, the value of the gold that was exported from West Africa far exceeded the value of the slaves until the eighteenth century. Finding something to exchange for these goods was always a problem for the Portuguese and to a lesser extent the northern Europeans who later dominated the trade. West Africans had been involved in trade with North Africa long before Europeans arrived and had certain tastes and expectations that Europeans had to satisfy. They had been buying cloth from North Africa, mostly high-end cloth used by elites. These elites typically found the European woolens unappealing, so the Portuguese were compelled to buy North African cloth and bring it to West Africa. In effect, they were selling their services as sailors, bringing the same cloth West Africans had been buying out of the trans-Saharan trade, but delivering it by a cheaper route. This sums up the Portuguese approach to trade. They made little that anyone else wanted. What they did have that other people wanted were firearms, which, for obvious reasons, they were hesitant to sell, and ships. They used their ships to move goods a bit more cheaply than anyone else could and used that profit to buy the African (or Asian) goods they wanted.

Just as the Portuguese did not create the West African cloth trade, so too they did not create the slave trade in Africa. Rather they reshaped and reoriented a preexisting slave trade toward new markets. Slaves had been traded across the Sahara for centuries prior to the arrival of Europeans in West Africa. There was also a small slave trade within West Africa that moved enslaved war captives and other types of slaves between West African societies. The Portuguese innovation was to use their ships to move these slaves to places that the older slave trade did not reach—the Atlantic islands and then the Americas. In doing so, they probably created new economic conditions that greatly increased the scale of the slave trade within Africa and quite possibly made the institution of slavery more brutal than it had been prior to their involvement in the trade.[2]

The influx of African slaves into Brazil and later into the Caribbean had a huge economic effect. By replacing Indian laborers, who were dying out and were legally protected from enslavement (though the law often yielded to economic pressure), and European laborers, who played a role in Barbados but enjoyed too many legal protections for their employers' comfort, Africans were coerced into producing sugar in such huge quantities that it became increasingly commonplace in Europe.

This development in the sugar trade left its mark on the entire Atlantic rim. We have discussed the dietary effects of this revolution on Europeans above, but the economic and social effects of sugar extended from New England to West Africa to Brazil to England. In New England, where a long maritime tradition sent sea captains to the West Indies and to West Africa, molasses became central to the economy and to people's diets. Molasses is a liquid byproduct of sugar-making that was exported from the West Indies to New England. Traditional New England foods—specifically brown bread and baked beans—are flavored with molasses. Molasses was added to livestock feed and even put in the water that horses and cows were given (sports drink for animals) to make the water more palatable and to prevent its freezing in the winter.

If the eighteenth century had a Hot Drinks Revolution, it also had a Distilled Drinks Revolution. Rum, which is distilled from fermented molasses, was at the forefront of that revolution, a distinction it shared with gin. New Englanders loved their rum. John Adams commented that "molasses was an essential ingredient in American independence," and he was not referring to Boston baked beans. New Englanders also made rum for export, sending it to Europe and to West Africa, where it was sometimes traded for slaves. Thus, sugar byproducts were traded for the very slaves needed to make the sugar industry work. If West Africans had a taste for rum, it paled in comparison with England. Rum, along with gin, was the first cheap distilled alcohol available in England. Whisky and imported brandy, made from barley and grapes respectively, were too expensive for the average drinker. Rum changed that and as a result the eighteenth century saw the democratization of dissipation. In the late eighteenth century, England imported over two million gallons of rum a year. The Royal Navy provided its sailors with a daily rum ration in the form of grog, which is rum cut with water.

In West Africa the sugar trade brought misery for those whose lives were disrupted by slavery, but also it also brought economic opportunity, and new forms of cultural innovation. Beginning in the fifteenth century, European merchants settled on the coast and they usually married locally. The result was mixed-race families of merchants in trading centers along the West African coast. These merchants were classic examples of the cross-cultural broker. They were European enough to deal comfortably with visiting European merchants, but also African enough to have access to local markets that the visitors could not hope to penetrate. They and many other Africans who lived in trading centers along the coast participated in an Atlantic World. They shared a cuisine with people of African descent in the New World, along with hair styles and taste in cloth and clothing. In addition to importing cloth, West Africans exported it, probably to the New World where uniquely West African types of cloth were sought by people of African descent. Probably the most important African contribution to the common culture of the tropical Atlantic was religious. West African religion crossed the Atlantic and may possibly have been shaped in turn by developments in the Americas. Religions that have their roots in West Africa are found wherever sugar was grown by African slaves. Brazil, Haiti, and Jamaica, all have religions that clearly derive from the Yoruba religious tradition. An interesting, but highly contentious case, has been made suggesting that the form the Yoruba religion now takes in Nigeria, in fact, owes something to the influence of Afro-Brazilians who returned to West Africa bringing with them an American version of Yoruba religion.

In the Americas, Africa's influence was profound. The number of Africans coming to the Americas was larger than the number of Europeans coming to the Americas until the nineteenth century. African religion, food, and music, to say nothing of the wealth generated by the labor of slaves, shaped the cultural development of parts of the Atlantic coasts of the Americas almost as much Europe did. The Caribbean and tropical Brazil are more African than anything else.

CONCLUSION

The sugar trade provides a window on Europe's changing role in world trade before the industrial revolution. A crop that was virtually unknown to Europeans in classical times and could not be grown in most parts of Europe became central to the diets and economies of Western Europe. By the eighteenth century, Europeans had not only learned to grow sugar cane, they had introduced it to new continents, moved people across oceans to grow it, developed new technologies to produce and transport it, and reshaped their eating and drinking habits around it. There is much debate about the role of the sugar industry in laying the ground for the industrial revolution. A prominent economic historian recently concluded that the sugar industry and its handmaiden the slave trade were not essential to the industrial revolution but probably accelerated the process. Whatever the effect of the sugar industry on the industrial revolution, it certainly foreshadowed the rise of Europe as a global economic power in the nineteenth century.

SOURCES

Portuguese Motives
Gomes Eannes de Azurara, *Chronicle of the Discovery and Conquest of Guinea*

As we have seen, the Portuguese played a crucial role in the creation of the Atlantic sugar industry also pioneered the creation of the sugar industry's companion, the Atlantic slave trade. It was Portuguese ships bringing African slaves from the West African coast to Lisbon and Madeira in the fifteenth century that marked the opening of a trade that would grow hand in hand with the sugar industry into the eighteenth century.

Gomes Eannes de Azurara's *Chronicle* provides a window on the motives of the Portuguese in this era. Azurara worked in the royal library of Portugal, and wrote several commissioned histories of the royal family's exploits. Finished in 1453, the *Chronicle,* describes Prince Henry the Navigator's (1394–1460) life and achievements. Henry played a central, though mostly organizational, role in the Portuguese voyages of discovery. Because he worked for the royal family, Azurara's account is probably an accurate reflection of Henry's own perception of his motives. Perhaps the most interesting feature of the passage that follows is its indifference to matters economic. Considering the economic implications of what they were doing, the Portuguese seem to downplay the economic importance of their explorations.

According to Azurara, did Henry send his ships to West Africa looking for slaves? What were they looking for? How believable is Azurara's account on this point? One of Azurara's earlier books was a history of the conquest in 1415 of Ceuta, a port in North Africa, an event that the Portuguese saw as an extension of the *reconquista,* or reconquest of the Iberian Peninsula from Islamic forces that became an integral part of Christian Europe's crusading ventures and lasted down to 1492. Do you see any evidence in this text that there was also an element of crusading to their ventures in Africa? What is Azurara's attitude toward Africans? How does he justify their enslavement? Does he seem sincere? What do you conclude from your study of this document after having addressed these questions?

Chapter VII: In which five reasons appear why the Lord Infant[3] was moved to command the search for the lands of Guinea.[4]
We imagine that we know a matter when we are acquainted with the doer of it and the end for which he did it. And since former chapters

we have set forth the Lord Infant[5] as the chief actor in these things, giving as clear an understanding of him as we could, it is appropriate that in this present chapter we should know his purpose in doing them. And you should note well that the noble spirit of this Prince, by a sort of natural constraint, was ever urging him both to begin and to carry out very great deeds ... [H]e always kept ships well armed against the Infidel,[6] both for war and because had also a wish to know the land that lay beyond the isles of Canary that Cape called Bojador,[7] for up to his time, neither by writings, nor by the memory of man, was known with any certainty the nature of the land beyond that Cape ... And because the said Lord Infant wished to know the truth of this—since it seemed to him that if he or some other lord did not endeavor to that knowledge, no mariner or merchants would ever dare to attempt it—(for it is clear that none of them ever trouble themselves to sail to a place where there is not a sure and certain hope of profit)—and seeing also that no other prince took any pains in this matter, he sent out his own ships against those parts to have manifest certainty of them all. And to this he was stirred up by his zeal for the service of God and the King Edward his Lord and brother who then reigned. And this was the first reason of his action.

The second reason was that if there chanced to be in those lands some population of Christians, or some havens into which it would be possible to sail without peril, any kinds of merchandise might be brought to this realm, which could find a ready market, and reasonably so, because no other people of these parts traded with them, nor yet people of any other that were known; and also the product of this realm might be taken there, which traffic would bring great profit to our countrymen.

The third reason was that, as it was said that the power of the Moors in that land of Africa was very much greater than commonly supposed, and that there were no Christians among them, nor any other race of men; and because every wise man is obliged by natural prudence to wish for knowledge of the power of his enemy; therefore the said Lord Infant exerted himself ... to make it known determinately how far the power of those infidels extended.

The fourth reason was because during the one and thirty years that he had warred against the Moors, he had never found a Christian king, nor a lord outside this land, who for the love of our Lord Jesus Christ would aid him in the said war. Therefore he sought to know if there were in those parts any Christian princes, in whom the charity and love of Christ was so ingrained that they would aid him against those enemies of the faith.

The fifth reason was his great desire to make increase in the faith of our Lord Jesus Christ and to bring to him all the souls that should be saved . . . For he perceived that no better offering could be made unto the Lord than this . . . For I who wrote this history saw so many men and women of those parts turned to the holy faith, that even if the Infant had been a heathen, their prayers would have been enough to obtain his salvation. And not only did I see the first captives but their children and grandchildren as true Christians . . .

But over and above these five reasons I have a sixth that would seem the root from which all the others proceed: and this is the inclination of the heavenly wheels . . . I wish to tell you how by the constraint of the influence of nature this glorious Prince was inclined to those actions of his. And that is because his ascendent was Aries, which is the house of Mars and exaltation of the sun . . . [*a long astrological discussion follows*] . . . signified that this Lord should toil at high and mighty conquests, especially in seeking out things that were hidden from other men and secret.

Sugar Production in Barbados
Richard Ligon, *A True and Exact History of the Island of Barbadoes*

Richard Ligon, an Englishman who lived in Barbados between 1647 and 1650, was in a position to observe the early stages of the sugar industry's move into the Caribbean and the functioning of England's first successful sugar colony. His book, published in 1657, is a general account of the island, covering everything from its topography to flora and fauna to social and economic conditions. The book contains a lengthy description of the process of sugar making and advice about techniques that will maximize sugar yields.

Perhaps the most notable feature of the work is its sunny optimism. Sugar planting was just beginning to produce large fortunes, and he included tables that show how a small investment in Barbados could make someone rich. Ligon's optimism extended to a cheerful indifference to the status of the slaves and indentured workers who cultivated the sugar.

Despite his optimism about sugar, Ligon suggests that the situation of planters in Barbados may have been a bit precarious. What precautions have they taken to prevent a slave uprising? Ligon's statements about the virtues of sugar are generally consistent with seventeenth-century views of it. Does his attitude toward sugar suggest that it was a high value trade good or a lower value commodity in his time? Does Ligon show any reticence or concern about the idea of sugar planters making large amounts of money? What does this tell us about the status of the commercial classes in seventeenth-century England?

On Slaves:

It has been accounted a strange thing, that the Negroes, being more than double the numbers of the Christians that are there, and they accounted a bloody people . . . that these should not commit some horrid massacre upon the Christians, thereby to enfranchise themselves,[8] and become masters of the Island. But there are three reasons that take away this wonder; the one is, they are not suffered[9] to touch or handle any weapon; the other is, that they are held in such awe and slavery, as they are fearful to appear in any daring act . . . a third reason, which stops all designs of that kind . . . They are fetched from several parts of Africa, and speak several languages, and by that means, one of them understands not another.

The early days of Barbadian sugar production:

At the time of our arrival there, we found many sugar works set up, and at work, but yet the sugars they made, were but muscavadoes,[10] and few of them merchantable commodities; so moist, so full of molasses, and so ill-cured, as they were hardly worth the bringing home for England. But about the time I left the island, which was in 1650, they were much bettered; for then they had the skill to know when the canes were ripe, which was not, till they were fifteen months old; and before they gathered them at twelve, which was a main disadvantage to the making of good sugar; for the liquor wanting of the sweetness it ought to have, caused the sugars to be lean, and unfit to keep . . . and now, seeing this commodity, sugar, has gotten so much the start of all the rest of the those, that were held the staple commodities of the land, and so much over topped them, as they are for the most part slighted and neglected . . . sugar making . . . is now grown the sole trade on this island.

On the virtues of Sugar:

I do think fit to give you a Saraband,[11] with my best touches as last; which shall be only this, that this plant [sugar cane] has a faculty, to preserve all fruits, that grow in the world, from corruption and putrefaction; so it has a virtue, being rightly applied, to preserve us men in our health and fortunes too. Doctor Butler, one of the most learned and famous Physicians that this Nation or world ever bred, was wont to say that,

> If sugar can preserve both our pears and plums,
> Why can it not preserve as well our lungs?

And that it might work the same effect on himself, he always drank in his Claret wine, great store of the best refined sugar, and also prescribed it in several ways to his patients, for colds, coughs, and catarrs;[12] which are diseases, that reign in cold climates, especially in Islands, where the air is moister than in continents; and so much for our health.

Now for our fortunes, they are not only preserved, but made by the powerful operation of this plant.

Colonel James Drax, whose beginning upon that Island, was founded upon a stock not exceeding 300 pounds sterling, has raised his fortune to such a height, as I have heard him say, that he would not look towards England, with a purpose to remain there, the rest of his life, till he were able to purchase an estate of ten thousand pound[s] land yearly; which he hoped in a few years to accomplish, with what he was the owner of; and all by this sugar plant . . . Now if such estates as these may be raised, by the well ordering of this plant, by industrious and painful men, why may not such estates, by careful keeping, and orderly and moderate expending, be preserved, in their posterities, to the tenth generation, and all by the sweet negotiation of sugar?

Sugar Slavery in Surinam
George Warren, *An Impartial Description of Surinam*

Published in 1667, George Warren's account of Surinam dates from the time when Surinam was briefly an English colony. Located on the northern coast of South America, Surinam and its neighbors the two Guyanas were early homes of the plantation complex in the New World. The same year Warren's account was published the British traded Surinam to the Dutch in exchange for New York. At the time most people thought the Dutch had gotten the better end of the deal. Sugar was a huge money maker; New York was less obviously a source of wealth.

The sugar industry in Surinam, under both the English and the Dutch, was associated with an unusually brutal approach to slavery. As had been the case on Sao Tome, the slaves from the sugar plantations in Surinam escaped in large numbers and, following the rivers into the interior, established maroon, or fugitive slave, societies. The maroons were a magnet for escaped slaves, but they also raided the plantations to carry off slaves for their own use.

Interestingly, almost nothing is known about George Warren, except that he wrote this book. The book follows many of the conventions in Ligon's, *True and Exact History,* in that it covers basically the same topics: climate, topography, flora, fauna, commerce, sugar, and slaves. Where it differs is that Warren does not share Ligon's sunny optimism. Where Ligon sees potential wealth, Warren just sees brutality.

Ligon distinguishes between slaves and Christians, and Warren plainly states that the slaves in Surinam were not Christians. This seems to be at odds with Azurara's justification of the slave trade. Why do you suppose that sugar planters might be reluctant to convert their slaves to Christianity? Or might it have been the slaves' preference to not adopt their masters' religion? In many ways, the mainland colonies like Surinam, with more rainfall and rivers that could be used for transportation, were better suited to sugar production than were islands like Barbados. But ultimately Barbados and other islands proved more successful. Does this account of slavery in Surinam suggest any reasons why this might be the case? Keeping in mind that this book was published 100 years before there was even a rudimentary abolitionist movement, what is Warren's attitude toward slavery in Surinam?

Chapter VII The Plantations:

Canes become fit to break in twelve months when they are about six foot high and as thick as a man's wrist: they bear a top like a flag, which being cut off, and the canes squeezed through a mill, the juice is boiled in coppers to a competent thickness, and then poured into wooden pots, made broad and square at the top, and tapered to the compass of a six-pence at the bottom with a hole through, which is stopped with a little stick, till the sugar begins to be cold and stiffened; when it is pulled out and by that passage, the molasses drains from it; and being cured a while after this manner, is knocked into hogsheads, and shipped off.

Chapter VIII Of the Negroes or Slaves

Who are most brought out from Guinea in Africa to those parts, where they are sold like dogs, and no better esteemed but for their work sake, which they perform all the week with the severest usages for the slightest fault, till Saturday afternoon, when they are allowed to dress[13] their own gardens of plantations, having nothing but what they produce from thence to live upon; unless perhaps once or twice a year, their masters vouchsafe them, as a great favor, a little rotten salt fish: or if a cow or horse die of itself, they get roast meat: their lodging is a hard board, their black skins their covering. These wretched miseries not seldom drive them to desperate attempts for the recovery of their liberty, endeavoring to escape, and, if like to be retaken, sometimes lay violent hands upon themselves; or if the hope of pardon bring them back again alive into their master's power, they'll manifest their fortitude, or rather obstinacy in suffering the most exquisite tortures can be inflicted upon then, for a terror and example to other without shrinking . . . [they] practice no religion there, though many of them are circumcised: But they believe the ancient Pythagorean error of the soul's transmigration out of one body into another,[14] that when they die, they shall return into their own countries and be regenerated, so live in the world by constant revolution; which conceit makes many of them over-fondly woo their deaths, not otherwise hoping to be freed from that indeed unequalled slavery.

Thomas Phillips, *Journal of a Voyage Made in the Hannibal 1694–4*

This is a description of the Atlantic slave trade by a participant. Thomas Phillips was the captain of the slave ship *Hannibal*. Phillips' voyage took him through the Canaries, Cape Verde, and most of the major trading ports of the West African coast. He left the coast after buying provisions at Sao Tome, a major landmark for both the sugar and slave trades. The excerpt below begins in the West African port of Whydah, where, after several months spent buying ivory and gold on other part of the coast, the *Hannibal* bought its cargo of slaves.

From whom did Phillips purchase his slaves? To what extent did Phillips set the terms under which he bought slaves in Whydah? How does Phillips perceive Africans? Does he see them as inferior to Europeans? Does Phillips have any qualms about his profession? Does your answer to this question make sense in light of your answer to the previous question? What does this suggest about seventeenth-century attitudes toward slavery in Europe? What sort of hazards did Europeans involved in the slave trade face? How did that compare with the hazards faced by the enslaved? How profitable was this particular voyage of the *Hannibal* for the Royal Africa Company? Be specific.

. . . the kings slaves were the first offered to sale, which the cappasheirs[15] would be very urgent with us to buy, and would in a manner force us to buy it ere they would show us any other . . . and we must not refuse them . . . and we paid more for them than any others, which we could not remedy, it being one of his majesties prerogatives; then the cappasheirs each brought out his slaves according to his degree and quality, the greatest first, etc. and our surgeon examined them well in all kinds, to see if they were sound [of] wind and limb, making them jump, stretch out their arms swiftly, looking in their mouths to judge their age; for the cappasheirs are so cunning, that they shave them all close so we can see no grey hairs in their heads or beards; and then having liquored them well and sleeked them with palm oil, 'tis no easy matter to know an old one from a middle-aged one, but by the teeths decay; but our greatest care of all is to buy none that are poxed, lest they should infect the rest . . . When we had selected from the rest such as we liked, we agreed what goods to pay for them, the prices already being stated before the king, how much of each sort of merchandise we should give for a man, woman, and child, which gave us much ease . . . then we marked the slaves we had bought in the breast, or shoulder, with a hot iron, having the ship's name on it, the place being before anointed with a little palm oil, which caused but little pain . . .

The negros are so willful and loth to leave their own country, that they have often leap out of the canoes, boat and ship, into the sea, and kept under water till they were drowned, to avoid being taken up and saved by our boats, which pursue them; they having a more dreadful apprehension of Barbados than we can have of hell, tho' in reality they live much better there than in their own country; but home is home.

. . . [they] are as much the works of God's hand, and no doubt as dear to him as ourselves; nor can I imagine why they should be despised for their color, being what they cannot help, and the effect of the climate it has pleased God to appoint them. I can't think there is any intrinsic value in one color more than another, nor that white is better than black, only that we think it so because we are so, and are prone to judge favorably in our own case, as well as the blacks, who in odium of the color, say, the devil is white, and so paint him.

[Referring to Saint Thomas as he calls Sao Tome] The town may contain about 200 White inhabitants, who all look like shadows, and seldom arrive at[16] the age of fifty years, tho' the negros which are in great numbers, agree well enough with the climate, which is so very malignant, that few or none of the Portuguese would come to live here but such as are forced to flee, or are banished [from] their country for some villanies . . . We spent in our passage from St. Thomas to Barbados two months eleven days . . . in which time there happened such sickness and mortality among my poor men and negros, that of the first we buried 14, and of the last 320, which was a great detriment to our voyage, the Royal Africa company losing ten pounds by every slave that died . . . I delivered alive to at Barbados to the company's factors 372, which being sold came out at about nineteen pounds per head with another.

NOTES

1. It is worth noting that the exact number is unknowable and is the source of a fierce scholarly debate. Suffice it to say that many died, and we will probably never know the exact numbers or the even percentages.
2. This is a hotly debated topic and has been for the last 30 years. Some scholars contend that the Portuguese merely tapped into an already significant slave trade in West Africa; others argue that slavery was virtually unknown before the arrival of Europeans.
3. Prince Henry. An *infante* was any son of a Portuguese or Spanish monarch who was not the first in line to the Crown.
4. A general term of the West Africa.
5. Henry.
6. Nonbelievers. Namely Muslims, who are, of course, not Christians.
7. A cape on the Atlantic coast of Africa in modern Mauritania.
8. To free themselves.
9. Allowed.
10. Coarse, unrefined sugar.
11. A type of dance, here in the sense of a grand finale.
12. Inflammations of the nose and throat.
13. To tend or cultivate.
14. The Pythagorean school of philosophy, founded in southern Italy in the sixth-century B.C.E. by the Greek thinker Pythagoras (circa 580–500 B.C.E.), taught that the immortal soul is imprisoned in a cycle of bodily rebirths until it is released through a process of purification, which is best achieved through study of nature and the cosmos.
15. A term that refers to the notables, or chiefs.
16. Live to.

CHAPTER

4

The Silk Trade

SILK PRODUCTION

Silk is an anomaly among the commodities that we are dealing with in this book. Unlike spices, salt, and sugar, silk has never lost its status as luxury good. While the world's silk supply has increased dramatically in the last 2,000 years, silk is still not cheap. It still is the fabric of choice when people want to make a statement. Silk pajamas are decadent in a way that plain old cotton pajamas will never be. This owes primarily to silk's remarkable qualities as a fiber and the labor-intensive difficulties of producing silk.

Silk is produced by twisting together the cocoon filaments of several varieties of silkworms into threads and then weaving the threads into cloth. There are several species of silkworms, but the worm that produces most of the world's silk is the caterpillar of the moth *Bombyx mori*. These appear to have been domesticated first in China, probably before 5000 B.C.E. The *Bombyx mori* moth has been domesticated so long that it does little except lay eggs. It is flightless and lives only a few days, during which time it mates and lays roughly 500 eggs, which must be collected and stored under carefully controlled temperatures. The temperature of the eggs is slowly raised until the eggs hatch. Once the eggs hatch into caterpillars they are fed finely chopped leaves of the mulberry tree. It will take 2,000 pounds of mulberry leaves to produce 12 pounds of silk because the silkworms feed voraciously, consuming 20 times their weight in leaves, as they store energy to produce their cocoon. By the end of a month, they are 10,000 times larger than at birth.

When they are ready to spin their cocoons they begin to lift up the front of their bodies and waggle from side to side. The alert silk grower notices this and transfers them to racks where each worm spins its cocoon. Once they have finished, they are killed because silk produced from cocoons damaged by hatching is vastly inferior. Traditionally the pupae were killed by being placed in the hot sun. During the Golden Age of Chinese Buddhism, however, some pious devotees, whose religion prohibits the killing of any sentient being, were known to sacrifice profit to principle by allowing the chrysalis, or pupa, to mature into a moth. The cocoons next have to be boiled in water and the silk filament unreeled. Each cocoon is made of a single filament that is between 500 and 1,200 yards long. Five to ten of these are combined to make a single thread of silk. It is these long single filaments that make silk so unusual. Unlike other natural fibers, where thousands of shorter fibers have to be spun together to make thread, silk's continuous filaments are what make it so strong and supple. This is why preventing the worms from hatching is so important; when they chew through the cocoon they cut the fiber into many shorter pieces rather than the much more desirable single long filament.

The resulting thread is remarkable stuff. It has 60 percent of the tensile strength of steel wire. It holds dye better than any other fiber, which is why silk fabrics are as lustrous as they are. People claim that silk clothing is cool in hot weather and warm in cool weather, and it wicks moisture away from the body. Perhaps the central reason that silk was and is so highly esteemed is because of the way it drapes. Silk fibers can be spun into finer thread than any other natural fiber. The drape of a fabric is largely determined by the number of threads per square inch. Finer threads yield better draping fabrics. A fabric such as denim that is made from coarse, thick fibers is stiff. A fabric made from finely spun fibers such as pima cotton or silk and woven at a high thread count will be soft and drapery. Long before it was possible to make high quality, luxury cottons, silk could be used to make brilliantly colored and finely woven cloth. As such it was the fabric of choice for people in much of Eurasia and Africa who wanted to make a sartorial statement.

The complexity of silk production originally served to slow the spread of silk growing from China to other lands. The imperial Chinese government attempted to prevent the spread of silk cultivation out of China, and perhaps its efforts slowed the spread of sericulture, but it seems more likely that the slow spread of silk production had more to do with the process itself and the sensitivity of the silkworms. There are any number of mythic stories about the subterfuges that were needed to bring the silkworm to new places. A Chinese princess is said to have hidden silkworm eggs and mulberry seeds in her hair in order to escape inspection by Chinese border officials as she traveled west to marry a Central Asian king (Figure 4.1). Apparently she could not bear to live without silk and so introduced sericulture to the kingdom of Khotan, which became a center of silk production as early as the fifth century C.E. Likewise, we are told that around the year 550 the Byzantine emperor Justinian dispatched two monks back to their home in Central Asia, possibly Khotan, with orders to bring him silkworms. They returned with silkworm eggs hidden inside their walking sticks and were richly rewarded. The result was the introduction of the silkworm to the eastern Mediterranean.

These stories fit reasonably well with the chronology of the spread of sericulture, but it seems far more likely that the main hindrance to its spread was the vast amount of knowledge and the need for a significant investment in (otherwise pretty useless) mulberry trees and bushes that slowed the expansion of sericulture. The traditional story about the spread of sericulture to Japan tells not of the arrival of the silkworm, but of a mission sent to China that brought back four young women who were experienced silk growers. It was the knowledge brought by these women that inaugurated silk growing in Japan. It is also worth noting that the variety of silkworm that produces Indian silk is different than the Chinese *Bombyx mori*, again suggesting that it was the spread of complex cultural techniques rather than silkworms themselves that let others begin to produce silk.

If others eventually learned to grow silk, they came to it much later than the Chinese. And, at least in the case of India, the local variety of silkworm produces inferior silk. China was the home of silk

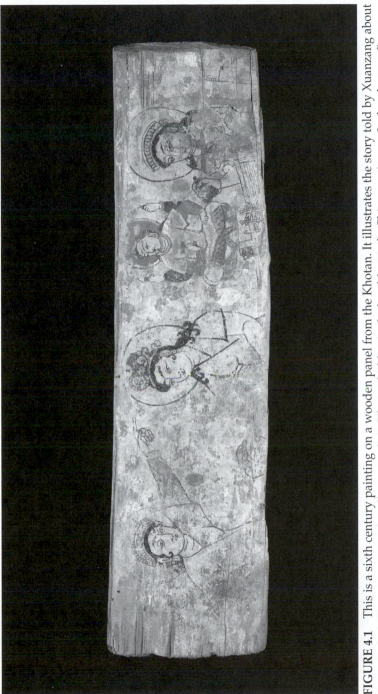

FIGURE 4.1 This is a sixth century painting on a wooden panel from the Khotan. It illustrates the story told by Xuanzang about the arrival of silkworm eggs and mulberry seeds in Khotan hidden in the headdress of a Chinese princess. It also shows a figure on the far right using a beating comb and a loom and another figure, between the princess and the weaver, who is the patron deity of weaving.

Source: © The British Museum.

cultivation and even after others learned to produce and weave it, they still imported large quantities of finished silk cloth and raw silk from China.

SILK IN CHINA

By 1750 silk was produced in Europe, India, the Middle East, and Central Asia, as well as China, but nowhere has silk come to have the depth of social meaning that it does in China. Silk was first produced in China, and over the last 7,000 years has played crucial roles in China's modes of dress, as well as its burial practices, religious observances, and art, and, of course, its economy. Simply put, silk is central to Chinese identity. In China the first person to cultivate the silkworm is supposed to have been the Lady Xiling Leizu, the wife of Huangdi, the Yellow Emperor—one of the mythical founders of China, who supposedly ruled from 2698 to 2598 B.C.E. She is also credited with the invention of the loom. Thus the origins of sericulture are seen as linked with the origins of China.

The earliest evidence for silk production in China dates from roughly 5000 B.C.E. Tools used for spinning and weaving have been found at Neolithic sites in northern China, but it is not certain that they were used for silk making rather than some other textile. (China was also at the forefront of hemp domestication and the production of ramie, which is a fiber made from nettles—probably as challenging to work with as silkworms, but for different reasons.) Nearby sites, which lack evidence of weaving equipment, have turned up carvings of silkworms, which suggests that North China had both silkworms and the weaving technology to produce silk cloth. Given the perishable nature of silk, there is not much more evidence than this for early silk production in China.

The oldest surviving piece of silk cloth comes from 3630 B.C.E. in North China. It was used as a burial shroud for a child, which points to the early association between silk and burial rituals. In China and elsewhere silk came to be used to wrap the dead and their grave goods, to adorn the tombs of Christian saints and the relics of the Buddha, and as clothing for the dead. An archaeological site that dates from the middle of the 3rd millennium produced further evidence of silk in Neolithic China. There archaeologists found several pieces of silk: a braided belt, silk threads used as ribbons, and a fragment of woven cloth. The woven cloth was a simple, plain weave (called "tabby"), but with an astonishingly high thread count. That is to say, the number of threads per square inch, a standard measure of the quality of cloth, was similar to that of modern cloth. So even before the first recognized Chinese imperial dynasty emerged, the technology needed to produce silk and to produce high quality cloth existed in China. Furthermore, silk's status as a fabric associated with burial ritual was established in Neolithic times.

China's first documented royal dynasty was the Shang (as opposed to the semi-legendary Xia dynasty that the Chinese identify as their first), which ruled the area around North China's Hwang He (Yellow River) from circa 1750 to about 1050 B.C.E. Shang society is noted for its "oracle bones." These were sheep scapulae and turtle shells on which questions were written. The bones were then heated and the cracks generated by the heating were used to determine an answer to the question. The characters on these oracle bones constitute the oldest known form of written Chinese. The ground around the presumed capital of the Shang—Anyang—is littered with oracle bones, and it was the discovery first of these artifacts and then the administrative center in Anyang that lifted the Shang from mythic ancestors of ancient China to an historical dynasty. Among the characters found on the oracle bones is the character for silkworm. Thus, the earliest known form of written Chinese contains references to silkworms. There are over 100 references to silk or silkworms in the oracle bones. There are also references in the oracle bones to a "silk spirit." The notion of a silk goddess, or spirit, may go back to Neolithic times, but the rites associated with a silk goddess were clearly present in Shang times.

That there was a silk goddess (and thereafter most Chinese silk deities were female, including Empress Xiling Leizu, who became China's principal silk goddess because she was the First Sericulturalist) points to the relationship between silk production in China and women. From at least the time of the Shang until the appearance of large silk factories staffed by paid male laborers during the Ming era (1368–1644), silkworm cultivation and silk weaving have been almost exclusively women's work. This was true at all social levels. For peasants in the Han period (202 B.C.E.–220 C.E.), it was said that "men plow and women weave." Aristocratic women did not tend the silkworms or weave themselves, but they did oversee production by female servants and slaves. Even in the palace, it was the empress who (at least in

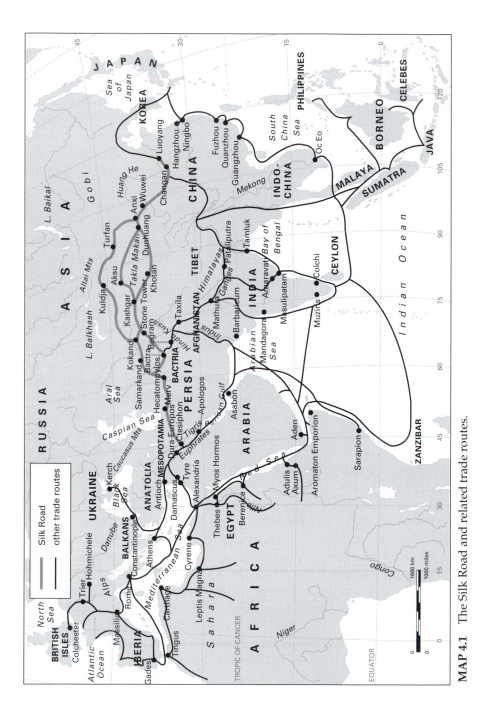

MAP 4.1 The Silk Road and related trade routes.

theory) managed the workshops which produced silk for the imperial household. Furthermore it was the empress' duty to carry out the rites associated with the veneration of the silk spirit. Even with the rise of large silk factories in the Ming era, silk production continued to be associated with women in the Chinese popular mind well into recent times, but as silk production spread out of China, that association, as we shall see, did not always hold.

Much of what is known about the Shang comes from the burials of Shang nobles. One of the duties of the Shang emperors was the veneration of their ancestors through ritual sacrifice. Upon their own deaths, they expected to join the ranks of the ancestors. As ancestors, they would need many of the same objects that they had used in life. Thus the tombs of Shang nobles were filled with grave goods that would serve the dead in the afterlife and also served to reflect their status in this life. Cast bronze vessels were used both in the ritual veneration of the ancestors and as grave goods. These bronze vessels also appear to have been routinely used in conjunction with silk cloth. Bronzes used as grave goods were wrapped in multiple layers of silk fabric. Bronzes used for ancestor veneration were either decorated with strips of silk cloth or had silk stretched across their tops to serve as a lid.

Bronze and jade (also used extensively for grave goods) when in contact with silk cloth for long periods of time acquire traces of the silk that wrapped them. Those traces, when studied under a microscope, allow archaeologists to detect not just the presence of silk, but the types of weaves used and even the pigments used to dye the cloth. By studying bronzes, archaeologists have learned that the Shang produced a number of different types of tabby weaves, as well as more looosly woven gauzes. Often the inner layer of a wrapping would be silk gauze. These textiles were being dyed with both mineral and vegetable dyes, which, because vegetable dyes are applied to the yarn before it is spun and mineral dyes must be applied to finished cloth, is a sign of the sophistication of Shang silk production.

It is also interesting to note that as early as the Shang era, there is sketchy evidence of the movement of silk to the west. A tomb in Xinjiang (now part of China, but then politically and culturally distinct) dating from 1100 B.C.E. contains silk fragments, which include the earliest known example of embroidered silk. Thus, even at this very early time, it appears that elites outside of China knew about and desired Chinese silk and that someone was bringing it to them. A sort of proto-Silk Road might date back to the end of the second millennium B.C.E. (Map 4.1).

The Shang were eventually supplanted by the Zhou (circa 1050–221 B.C.E.). Several crucial innovations in silk production took place during the Zhou period. In terms of production, embroidery became far more common and sophisticated. Perhaps most important, it was during the Zhou era that Chinese weavers learned to make patterned silk cloth (Figure 4.2). This is done with a much more complex loom than is used for making simple tabbies. The draw looms (a technology greatly elaborated during the Han era) used for making patterned silks enabled weavers to make cloths that had repeating patterns using many different colors of thread. The result was cloth that was different from plain tabby both in its texture and color patterns. Not surprisingly it was considered more desirable and, hence, more valuable.

A second development from the end of the Zhou era (the time known as the Warring States Period) is the use of silk as a writing material. Silk cloth is durable, it takes ink well, and can be rolled into scrolls without cracking or creasing. Thousands of silk scrolls recording Buddhist scripture on them have been recovered from the oasis towns of Central Asia. Silk would eventually become the preferred medium for Chinese painters and calligraphers. The first known use of silk in this role is from the southern Chinese state of Chu in the fourth century B.C.E.

Yet another interesting development of the Zhou era was the use of silk as a currency. The Zhou, like the Shang, made extensive use bronze vessels, but unlike the Shang they inscribed them with records of important events. The first-recorded instance of the use of silk as currency appears on a Zhou bronze that refers to the purchase of horses with silk. Later, in the Han era (202 B.C.E.–220 C.E.), it was routine for the imperial government to bribe steppe nomads with silk cloth, and within the empire, the Han government collected silk as payment for taxes and paid the salaries of imperial officials in silk.

The use of silk in the payment of tribute and salaries and the centrality of silk clothing and cloth in imperial ritual gave the Chinese state a strong interest in silk production. This led the Qin and the Han imperial dynasties, both much more centralized than the Zhou, to create a bureaucracy devoted to monitoring the production of silk. The short-lived Qin empire (221–206 B.C.E.) set a new standard in China for centralized rule. Its founder, Qin Shihuang Di, exerted state control over everything from weights and measures, to cart axle lengths, to musical scales, to tax collection. So perhaps it is not surprising that

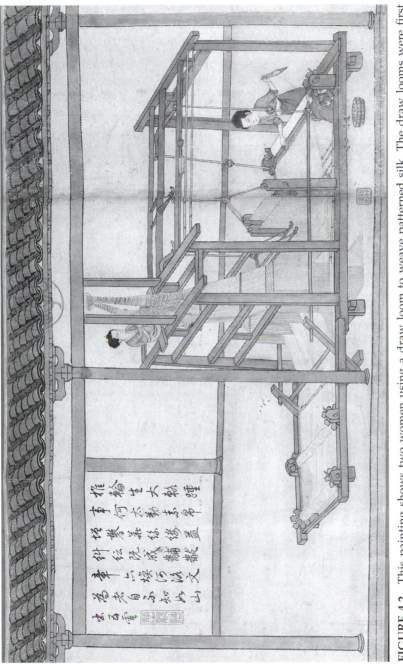

FIGURE 4.2 This painting shows two women using a draw loom to weave patterned silk. The draw looms were first developed in Han China, allowing complicated patterns to be woven into silk cloths.

Source: Emperor Hui Tsung, Chinese, 1082–1135. Ladies Preparing Newly Woven Silk, Part II. Chinese scroll painting, Sung Dynasty. Courtesy, Museum of Fine Arts, Boston. Reproduced with permission. © 2006 Museum of Fine Arts, Boston. All Rights Reserved.

he also brought at least part of China's silk production under state control. Under the Qin, two official workshops were created to supply the palace with silk. Laborers in the official workshops went through state-mandated apprenticeships and produced cloth to rigidly defined standards.

When the Han succeeded the Qin in 202, they retained and elaborated many of Qin's administrative practices. They continued to use government workshops to produce silk, and did so on a much larger scale than had the Qin. Under the Han, the imperial workshops produced thousands of silk cloths and garments each year and employed thousands of people, many of them slaves. The Han empress was in charge of the silk production within the imperial household and responsible for conducting the annual silkworm rites. The Chinese state's interest in silk is indicative of the importance of silk in the exercise of political power in imperial China. Silk's practical and symbolic roles were too important to be left to the whims of the market. As silk production spread to other regions, most notably to the Byzantine empire, there would be similar state-directed efforts to control silk production. It is worth noting that although the Qin and the Han put considerable effort into controlling silk production, they did not prevent private producers from making silk cloth. In fact, under the Han, silk production became widespread in both noble and peasant households. The result was widespread use of silk. By the end of the Han period, even peasants were wearing silk, though much plainer silks than the elaborately textured and colored cloth that their social betters wore.

During the Han period people outside of China became increasingly aware of Chinese silk and began to desire it more intensely than they had before. At the same time China was also growing more aware of the existence of the lands to the west and interested in the products that those lands had to offer them. The result was the opening of regular and sustained trade across Eurasia for the first time, and silk played a significant role in that trade.

ORIGINS OF THE SILK ROAD

When the Han came to power, China already had a long history of trade and conflict with the peoples of the Eurasian steppe. The horse nomads who inhabited the grasslands to the north and west of China had always been a problem for the agrarian regions of China. They found the wealth produced by the Chinese powerfully attractive. Sometimes they sought the Chinese goods they wanted through trade, and sometimes they raided for it. It was common practice for Chinese governments to try to pay off the nomads, to prevent their raiding into China. The tribute offered by the Chinese to the steppe nomads was substantial, and, as already noted, much of it was paid in silk. Eventually bolts of silk came to serve many of the functions of a currency on the steppes. Some of this silk was used by nomadic leaders to reward their followers and to create alliances, but some was used for trade.

Steppe nomads had two things that the Chinese wanted—furs and ponies—and they were happy to sell both to the Chinese. Consequently, there was a brisk trade along the frontier in which the nomads bartered their squat, sturdy tarpan ponies for Chinese goods, especially silk. But even with these ponies Chinese armies were hard-pressed to defend the northwest frontier against the same nomads who raided as well as traded.

A combined desire to know more about their nomadic adversaries and a search for allies against the nomad threat drove various Chinese emperors to send emissaries and explorers out into the steppe lands. The most famous of these was Zhang Qian. Han Wudi, the greatest of the Han emperors, came to power in 141 B.C.E. In 139/138 he sent Zhang Qian to seek allies against the biggest and most hostile of the steppe confederacies, a people the Chinese called the Xiongnu. Zhang Qian was the sort of man that emperors dream of. Captured shortly after he arrived on the steppe, he spent over 10 years with the Xiongnu as a slave. When he got the opportunity to escape he did not return to China, but continued his journey to the west. He eventually made it all the way to the regions of Bactria (in modern Afghanistan) and Ferghana (in modern Uzbekistan and Kyrgystan). There he failed to find allies but found evidence of trade with China. Furthermore he learned about the lands of India and Persia and the commercial possibilities there. From Han Wudi's perspective one of the most important discoveries from this journey was that there were superior horses in the Western Lands. These were the famous blood-sweating horses of Ferghana, which the Chinese called "heavenly horses" and also "dragon horses," out of a belief that their bleeding (probably the consequence of a parasite) and great size and speed were indications of their celestial origins and kinship with dragons.

These powerful steeds, far stronger and faster than the ponies of the steppe nomads along China's frontier, certainly caught imperial attention, and over time, ownership of these horses came to be considered a major status symbol in China. More immediately, Han Wudi organized a military expedition devoted to acquiring these horses. This amounted to a giant horse rustling expedition, but it had long-term consequences. It extended Han military power deep into Central Asia and created a safe route from China to Central Asia. The result was the "opening" of the Silk Road. Han protection made it easier for Central Asian merchants to travel to China, or for Chinese merchants to make the journey to Central Asia, and no doubt both happened. But it was probably the Central Asians, especially an Eastern Iranian people known as the Sogdians, who really pioneered these routes. In general, it is the peoples in the less economically developed places who make the long journeys to bring raw material (horses and such) to economically more central places. It might have been Han Wudi who created the political and military conditions that made the Silk Road possible, but it was anonymous Central Asians who actually traveled the long dusty paths and roads across Asia.

The other crucial factor in the opening of the Silk Road was the large scale assertion of imperial power in Eurasia. By the first century C.E., the Romans had consolidated their hold over the Mediterranean, the Han ruled an expanded China, and the Parthians had conquered and consolidated major portions of the old Persian empire. Rome shared a border with the Parthians, and Han outposts in Central Asia reached nearly to the eastern edges of Parthian control. The Khushan empire also emerged during this period stretching from northern India into Central Asia and acting as an intermediary between Parthia and China. So it was possible to cross Eurasia from Spain to the Yellow River and spend most of the journey under the laws and protections of one of the major empires. But rarely, if ever, did a single merchant make the trek from one end to the other during this first age of the Silk Road. Rather goods passed from hand to hand along the caravan routes and sea lanes that connected these four empires.

The stage was set for one of the great economic and cultural exchanges in human history. Chinese silk as well as other luxury goods were transported as far west as the Mediterranean, while Roman glassware, Indian spices and drugs, and Central Asian horses made their way to China. While this so-called Silk Road was clearly a major thoroughfare for trade and elites at both ends eagerly sought the rarities that it brought, its real economic significance is hard to judge. In many respects what is most remarkable about the trade in silk is the extent to which it served as a vector for the transmission of ideas. The Silk Road brought China its first taste of Buddhism, Christianity, Manichaeism, and Islam. It also spread Greco-Roman aesthetic ideas and even myths across Central Asia and even to China. The Silk Road also brought increased quantities of silk to places far beyond China, and eventually sericulture itself spread along the Silk Road. And just as the religions that spread along the Silk Road were transformed in their travels, so too silk came to be used for new purposes as it came to be more widely available outside of China.

ROMAN SILK

The expansion of trade to the west in the Han era, brought Chinese silk to the Roman Empire. The Roman naturalist Pliny the Elder (d. 79 C.E.), wrote about the use of silk in the Roman Empire. Just as Pliny (whom we met before in the spice chapter) thought Roman citizens were bankrupting the Empire with their taste for pepper, he did not approve of their love of silk. In Pliny's time Chinese silk appears to have been extremely rare, so rare that it was used primarily in small pieces to decorate linen or woolen garments. It was used for this purpose because of the way it took dye, especially the prized and rare murex purple. Purple cloth had long been the most prized color of cloth in the Mediterranean world. The process for making purple dye was first discovered by a Phoenician god, or so we are told, and the color has long been associated with religious and political authority. The ancient Hebrews were enjoined in Exodus to use purple cloth in the construction of the tabernacle. Roman emperors wore purple. Indeed the right to wear robes that were all purple was reserved to the emperor and occasionally to favored generals. Members of the Roman senate were allowed to wear purple trim on their togas, and victorious generals who were awarded a triumph were given tunics that had purple on them.

The reason purple had such powerful symbolic meaning was that making purple dye was exceedingly difficult. The dye was manufactured from a mollusk called "murex" which contains a small quantity of purple pigment that it releases when crushed. In order to make dye, "purple fishers" had to gather thousands of these creatures.

They were then crushed and the colored liquid gathered. This then had to be reduced by boiling for ten days. The resulting dye made a brilliant purple, but worked best with a white fabric. Chinese silk, which was white or off-white in its natural form, was the ideal fabric to use with murex purple. Thus, in the Mediterranean World, silk took on many of the same connotations of religious and political significance that it had in China, partly because of the inherent appeal of silk, but also because it was so well-suited to the purple dyes that were already established as status markers.

Pliny was not only concerned about the high cost of silk. There were moral considerations, too. Silk was being woven into light gauzy fabrics, so transparent that their wearers appeared—to Pliny anyway—to be naked. He seems especially disturbed that men, in addition to women, were also starting to wear these gauzy fabrics, a development that struck him as hopelessly effete. The way in which Pliny describes how this cloth is produced suggests that the Romans may have been unraveling Chinese silks and reweaving them more loosely.

It may also be that the silks which offended Pliny's sense of decency were the product of an indigenous silk weaving industry in Mesopotamia and on the Aegean island of Cos. Both of these industries relied on wild silks. These are silks made from cocoons gathered in the wild. These cocoons are produced by various members of the Bombyx genus, though they and their cocoon are quite different from the domestic Bombyx mori. The cocoons were gathered after the moth had escaped from the cocoon, so the single strand of silk from which the cocoon is made had been cut into many small filaments as the moth chewed its way out. Silk produced from wild cocoons must be carded and spun into a thread, unlike domestic silk which is simply unreeled from the cocoon in one long filament. Thus the strength and fineness of the fibers is greatly reduced. Furthermore these silks are usually dark in their natural state and thus do not take dye as well as Chinese domestic silk. Roman authors referred to these silks as "bombycina" rather than "sericum" the term they used for Chinese silk. According to tradition, the person who discovered this process was a woman named Pamphile, suggesting an interesting parallel with the Chinese association between silk production and women.

Interestingly, Pliny and other Romans authors understood that bombycina cloth was produced from the cocoons of moths, but believed that Chinese silk was a plant product. According to Pliny, silk was harvested from trees by a people called the Seres who soaked leaves in water and then combed off the down from the leaves to make silk. This may be either a garbled reference to the role of mulberry trees and the boiling of the cocoons in the silk-making process, or to cotton, which the Romans imported from India, or possibly to ramie or kapok. Pliny's confusion about the Seres is paralleled by China's equally vague knowledge of Rome. The Chinese had a name for the Romans, Da Qin, and knew a bit about their commercial desires and habits (including their use of wild silks), but other than that, very little mutual knowledge accompanied the silk that came from China to Rome in the first and second centuries C.E.

SILK PRODUCTION OUTSIDE OF CHINA

The trade on the Silk Road was a vehicle for many types of cultural exchange. In addition to the religious and aesthetic ideas that moved along the trade routes, so did the knowledge of how to produce silk. The first such westward movement was the spread of sericulture into Khotan in modern Xinjiang, circa 500 C.E. This is the event commemorated in the story of the princess who hid the silkworm eggs and mulberry seeds in her hair. Once silk production spread out of China to Khotan its spread to other regions of the Old World was rapid. In some cases the spread of sericulture built on local silk weaving industries that had relied on yarn imported from China. In both the Sassanian and Byzantine Empires, silk weaving long predated the production of domestic silk.

In Byzantium, it was in that reign of the Emperor Justinian (527–565) that sericulture was introduced. It was he who is said to have sent the two monks on the mission of commercial espionage mentioned at the beginning of the chapter. He did this because the Byzantine silk weaving industry depended on yarn purchased from the Sassanians. The Sassanians produced their own silk and also controlled access to Chinese silk. Not only did the Sassanians charge exorbitant prices, they were Byzantium's main military rival. Thus, Justinian's effort to obtain silkworms had strategic, as well as economic, implications.

Silk production did not initially increase all that much after the Byzantines became producers, as well as weavers, of silk. Justinian and his successors placed so many restraints on the silk industry that its growth was slow. But over the next few centuries silk production became an important part of the Byzantine economy. The Byzantine

Empire made a concerted effort to maintain its control over the production of silk cloth, but these were limited by the size of the empire and the steady decline of imperial control over the more distant provinces. By the eleventh and twelfth centuries the Greek city of Thebes was a major center of silk production and purple dying. Much of the southern Greek region of the Peloponnesus was planted with mulberry trees. Much of the silk production in this region seems to have occurred in defiance of the imperial monopoly.

Byzantine silk was produced for use by elites within the empire, but some of it was also exported to the Latin West. Venetian and Genoese merchants bought silk from the Byzantines, and from the Muslim caliphates, to meet the growing demand in Western Europe for silk cloth. Some of the silk that western Europeans bought was for the usual luxury clothing market, but much was intended for religious purposes. The rise of the Salvation religions caused a change in the meaning of and uses for silk all over Eurasia.

Silk and the Salvation Religions

The salvation religions have an interesting relationship with silk. Christianity, Mahayana Buddhism, Manichaeism, and Islam emphasize the salvation of individual souls. Saved souls live on in a blissful afterlife, while the less fortunate suffer torment in the next life. These religions are different from earlier religions in that they give priority to the next life rather than the present one, in their egalitarianism, and in their claim to a universal mission. Whereas a few earlier religions offered a type of blissful afterlife to the great and even the less well-born good, these not only opened up the possibility of an afterlife to those lowest on the social totem pole, they argued that wealth and power were more likely to be a hindrance to spiritual virtue than a benefit. Interestingly, the Silk Road seems to have played a role in the creation of these religions and clearly played a role in the movement of these religions across Eurasia.

The best example of this is Mahayana Buddhism, which, drawing upon ideas and movements already alive in the Buddhist Sangha, or community, became a significant force within the Khushan empire around the first century C.E. Khushana was the cultural cross roads of Asia. Its empire included portions of India, Persia, and Central Asia, and it was major player in trans-continental trade. This brought together people from all over Eurasia, who, adapting notions of salvation and salvation deities that were already popular in Southwest

Asia, devised a new form of Buddhism—the Mahayana, or Greater Vehicle, Doctrine, with its multiple savior Buddhas and bodhisattvas. Mahayana Buddhism then followed the trade routes out of the Khushan empire into Persia and India and then across central Asia into China and eventually to Korea and Japan.

The salvation religions forced people to think in new ways about silk. All of them preached that this life was little more than a precursor to a much more important next life. The wealth one might accrue in this life was trivial compared to the eternity of bliss or torment that awaited one in the next life. This posed a challenge to silk's role as a marker of wealth and social status. To be sure, the market for luxury goods never disappeared; then, as now, people were too good at rationalizing their desires for that to have happened. But it did open up some new uses for silk.

For Buddhists, silk was a means for making contributions to monasteries or shrines. One of the crucial differences between Mahayana and previous forms of Buddhism is that Mahayana places greater emphasis on the worship of the Buddha (actually, various Buddhas) and his (their) attendant bodhisattvas. The Lotus Sutra, a Mahayana scripture, calls on believers to honor the Buddha's shrines with the "seven treasures" (various precious metals and minerals) and silk decorations. Buddhists might honor the Buddha by donating these items to monasteries and stupas (domed shrines that held relics of the Buddha). Often the recipients of these donations lived far from the donors. Thus, when the Chinese Buddhist monk Xuanzang made his pilgrimage to India in the early seventh century, patrons along the way loaded him down with so much wealth that 30 horses were needed to carry it all. When a Tang emperor wanted to obtain a relic of the Buddha in 661, he sent 4,000 bolts of silk to a monastery in what is now Kabul to obtain it.

The silks donated to monasteries took several forms. Sometimes, as in the case above, it was bolts of plain tabby silk. This was probably intended as a store of wealth or raw material from which decorations could be made. Donors also sent robes for the officials and priests at the monasteries. They sent silk sutra covers—decorative sleeves used to store the scrolls on which the sutras were written (often on silk). Perhaps the most dramatic of the silk items presented to monasteries were elaborate silk banners that were displayed on the wall of the monasteries during religious holidays. These were made of several different pieces of cloth, often of different colors, and they made an inspiring sight—just as they do today at Buddhist shrines.

Christians were similarly conflicted about wealth. One way for wealthy Christians to mitigate the spiritual harm of their wealth was to donate it to religious causes, and as was the case with Buddhism, those donations often involved silk. Medieval European and Byzantine Christians found several uses for silk. One was for altar cloths. As more and more churches were constructed in Europe, the demand for silk coverings for their altars grew. Silk was also used for the ritual vestments worn by priests and bishops. Another use for silk was as wrappings for the relics of saints. The Christian veneration of saints' relics parallels the Buddhist veneration of the Buddha's relics. Christian saints' relics were often wrapped in silks, and the tombs of the kings and bishops, who were often interred in churches near the relics of saints, were likewise draped in silk.

For Europeans and the East Asians, this represented a major shift in burial practice. Early Chinese evidence for the use of silk comes almost entirely from graves. The dead were buried with their wealth. Wealthy Romans and the chiefs of the Germanic tribes were likewise buried or cremated with their wealth, and often in silk shrouds or clothing. But the salvation religions taught that no amount of wealth could replace spiritual virtue. Thus wealth that might once have been buried with the rich and powerful was instead donated to religious institutions. The result was the steady growth in the wealth of churches and monasteries all over Eurasia.

Western Europe initially purchased most of its silks from the Byzantine empire. But the Byzantines tried to prevent the export of their best silks. In the tenth century, Bishop Liuprand of Cremona tried to leave the Byzantine empire with some purple silk. It was confiscated by Byzantine customs officials, despite his protestations that it was to be used in his church. The Byzantine reluctance to export their finest silks, forced western Europeans to turn to other sources. Ironically it was the Islamic world that ended up supplying the churches of Western Europe with silk.

In the seventh century, Muslim armies overran much of the Byzantine Empire and all of the Sassanian Empire. As a result, they inherited a silk industry. Islam was, if anything, even more wary of silk than the other Salvation religions. Islamic law forbade men from wearing more than a two-inch strip of silk. In exemplary salvation-religion fashion, Muslims were promised silk garments in paradise, but enjoined to avoid them in this life. Despite this ambivalent attitude toward silk, the Muslim caliphate encouraged the growth of the silk industry. Both Sassanian and Byzantine silk production had been closely controlled by the state, so the Caliphate inherited not just a silk industry but one accustomed to direction from above. They directed the silk workshops to continue their work, but ordered that verses from the Quran be embroidered into the edges of the finer silks. These silks, called *tiraz* silks, were widely traded in the Mediterranean and many, along with their Quranic inscriptions, ended up in Christian churches.

Latin Christendom's growing wealth in the period between 1000 and 1500 meant a steady expansion of the market there for silk. Some of this was met by the importation from the Byzantine and Islamic worlds. But increasingly during this period, Europeans began to produce their own silk. At first this meant simply local embroidering of imported tabbies. But by the thirteenth century there were silk industries in Italy and France that relied on imported yarn, but prepared the thread and wove cloth locally. The process of making the thread is called "throwing" and the artisans who do it are called "throwsters." Silk throwing is a highly skilled craft, and silk throwsters and their guilds became an economically and politically important force in the cities where they lived. Silk production, rather than just the weaving of imported yarn, was introduced to southern France when the papacy moved to the French city of Avignon in the fourteenth century. By 1600 there were 10,000 looms in France used by silk weavers, and demand for silk yarn was so high that even though silk production was widespread in France, much of the yarn they used had to be imported. Silk weaving spread to England in 1685 when the French Crown ended its policy of tolerating Protestants, and many of them fled to Protestant countries. Many French Protestants had been involved in the silk industry, so their migration spread silk weaving all over Europe.

By 1750, silk was not only used but produced from one end of Eurasia to the other. Mulberry trees and silkworms were found from Japan to France. Silkworms had even been introduced, with limited success, in the Americas. Silk cloth wrapped the relics of saints and Buddhas, adorned the walls of monasteries and altars of churches, and covered the bodies of the well-dressed from Beijing to Delhi to Paris. Unlike sugar, spice, or salt, which by 1750 had lost their status as luxury goods, silk was still a precious and expensive thing in 1750. Even now, when silk is as cheap as it has ever been, silk makes a statement in a way that no other fiber does. A brightly colored silk scarf might cost three hundred dollars or more and makes a great anniversary present. A brightly colored cotton scarf is just a bandana.

SOURCES

Silk in the Roman World
Pliny the Elder, *Natural History*

Here Pliny, whom we met earlier in the spice chapter, discusses the sources of purple dyes, the murex shell, and the origins of silk. As was the case with his account of the origins of the various spices, he was a bit confused about the nature of silk. While he probably gives an accurate account of the Mediterranean wild-silk industry, he believes that Chinese silk is a plant product. He includes his account of the Seres, who are either the Chinese or Central Asian intermediaries in the silk trade, in Book VI, the part of his *Natural History* devoted to botany. His account of the Mediterranean silk industry comes from Book XI, which is devoted to insects and the organs of larger animals. Interestingly, silkworms are placed between the bees and hornets and the spiders, because bees and hornets build nests and hives and spiders also make silk. It is a long way to Linnaeus.

A reading of this document reveals Pliny's confusion as to the origins of Chinese silk. What other textile fiber might he be confusing it with? What did the Romans do with Chinese silk? Is the Romans' interest in silk a wholesome thing in Pliny's mind? Why or why not? Does the use of silk seem to have been widespread in Pliny's time?

Book VI
XX   . . . The first human occupants are the people called the Seres, who are famous for the woolen substance obtained from their forests; after soaking in water they comb off the white down of the leaves, and so supply our women with the double task of unraveling the threads and weaving them together again . . . so manifold the labor employed and, and so distant the region of the globe drawn upon, to enable the Roman matron to flaunt transparent raiment in public.

Book XI
LIII   But why do I mention these trifles [oysters and murex] when moral corruption and luxury spring from no other source in greater abundance than from the genus of shellfish? It is true that of the whole of nature the sea is most detrimental to the stomach in a multitude of

ways. . . . But what proportion do these form when we consider purple and scarlet robes and pearls . . . are we not content to feed on its dangers without being clothed with them?

XXV   Among these [the hornets] is a fourth genus, the silk-moth, which occurs in Assyria;[1] it is larger than the kinds mentioned above. Silk-moths make their nests of mud like a sort of salt; they are attached to a stone, and are so hard that they can scarcely be pierced with javelins. In these nests they make combs on a larger scale than bees do, and then produce a bigger grub.

XXVI   These creatures are also produced in another way. A specially large grub changes into a caterpillar with two projecting horns of a peculiar kind, and then into what is called a cocoon, and this turns into a chrysalis and this in six months into a silk-moth. They weave webs like spiders, producing a luxurious material for women's dresses, called silk [*bombycina*]. The process of unraveling these and weaving the thread again was first invented in Cos[2] by a woman named Pamphile, daughter of Plateas, who has the undeniable distinction of having devised a plan to reduce women's clothing to nakedness.

XXVII   Silk-moths are also reported to be born in the island of Cos . . . small butterflys are produced that are bare of down, and then as they cannot endure the cold they grow shaggy tufts of hair and equip themselves with thick jackets against the winter, scraping together the down of leaves with roughness of their feet; this is compressed by them into fleeces. . . . Then (they say) they are taken away by a man, put in earthenware vessels and reared with warmth and a diet of bran; but tufts of wool plucked off are softened in moisture and then thinned out into threads with a rush spindle. Nor even have men been ashamed to make use of these dresses, because of their lightness in summer: so far have our habits departed from wearing a leather cuirass that even a robe is considered a burden! All the same we so far leave the Assyrian silk-moth to women.

A Chinese Buddhist Pilgrim along the Silk Road
Xuanzang, *Record of the Western Regions*

Xuanzang (596–664) was one of the great Chinese Buddhist pilgrims and scholars of the Tang period. He became a novice Mahayana Buddhist monk at the age of 13 and spent much of his early life traveling through China seeking religious instruction. In 629, inspired by his reading of the works of Faxian, who had traveled to Indian 200 years earlier, he decided to visit the "western regions" to seek further religious instruction, relics, images of the Buddha, and sutras (Buddhist religious texts). His route took him across central Asia and into the northern India where he visited many Buddhist monuments and monasteries. He returned in 645, bringing relics of the Buddha, statues of the Buddha, 124 Mahayana sutras (scripture), and an additional 22 horse loads of other scriptures. Upon his return he translated many of these texts and published an account of his travels.

Xuanzang made his pilgrimage at a time when Buddhism had made its transition to a salvation religion, and when Buddhist monasteries were becoming repositories of wealth. His descriptions of places he visits include many brief references to the use of silk as decoration, and he gave gifts of silk to his hosts. He is also the source of the story about the spread of silkworms and mulberry trees to Khotan, the first known movement of silk production out of China. In this excerpt Khotan is called "Kustana."

Buddhists are not permitted to take life. What accommodations to this rule had the Buddhist silk makers in Khotan made? What effect might this have had on the quality of their silk? What does this story tell us about the relationship between China and silk? Why was this princess so anxious not to live in a land without silk? Does Xuanang seem bothered that the Celestial Kingdom was duped like this? What does this story tell us about the way China's neighbors saw the eastern kingdom?

In the old time this country [Khotan] knew nothing about mulberry trees or silkworms. Hearing that the eastern country[3] had them they sent an embassy to seek for them. At this time the prince of the eastern kingdom kept the secret and would not give possession of it to any. He kept guard over his territory and would not permit either the seeds of the mulberry or the silkworms' eggs to be carried off.

The king of Kustana sent off to seek a marriage union with a princess of the eastern kingdom, in token of his allegiance and submission. The king [of China] being well affected to the neighboring states acceded to his wish. Then the king of Kustana dispatched a messenger to escort the royal princess and gave the following direction: "Speak thus to the eastern princess. Our country has neither silk nor silken stuffs. You had better bring with you some mulberry seeds and silkworms, then you can make robes for yourself."

The princess, hearing these words, secretly procured the seed of the mulberry and the silkworms' eggs and concealed them in her head-dress. Having arrived at the barrier, the guard searched everywhere, but he did not dare to remove the princess' headdress. Arriving then in the kingdom of Kustana . . . they conducted her in great pomp to the royal place. Here then they left the silkworms and mulberry seeds.

In the spring time they set out the seeds, and when the time for the silkworms had come they gather leaves for their food; but from their first arrival it was necessary to feed them on different kinds of leaves, but afterwards the mulberry trees began to flourish. Then the queen wrote on a stone the following decree, "It is not permitted to kill the silkworm! After the butterfly has gone then the silk may be twined off [the cocoon]. Whoever offends against this rule may be deprived of divine protection." From old time until now this king-dom has possessed silkworms, which nobody is allowed to kill, with a view to take away the silk stealthily. Those who do are not allowed to rear the silkworms for a succession of years.

The Fourteenth-century Road to China
Francesco Pegolotti, *The Practice of Commerce*

Pegolotti wrote this account of the overland route from Europe to China around 1340, toward the end of the period during which China lay under Mongol rule. Although he never made the journey himself, as an employee of the House of Bardi, an Italian banking family, he was able to garner enough information from others to write this work. His book was a guide book for merchants, a sort of medieval *Lonely Planet* guide, that gave China-bound merchants from the West, especially Italy, detailed information about what to expect on the route east. It is a rare example of a merchant's perspective on the world of the Silk Road. Probably many other such documents were created in Europe and else-where, but because they contained valuable commercial intelligence they were kept private and have not survived into the present. Most of the book consists of list of products and prices, but it also has a short narrative, which we excerpt below.

What cultural accommodations does Pegolloti suggest that merchants make to easy their transit across Asia? What does it tell you about the volume and regularity of trans-Eurasian trade that Pegolotti was able to write this work, without having made the journey himself? How central is silk to the trade system that Pegolotti describes? Compare this with descriptions of the spice trade in Chapter 2.

In the first place you must let your beard grow long and not shave. And at Tana[4] you should furnish yourself with a dragoman.[5] And you must not try to save money in the matter of dragomen by taking a bad one instead of a good one. For the additional wages of the good one will not cost you so much as you will save by having him. And besides the dragoman it will be well to take at least two good menservants, who are acquainted with the Cumanian[6] tongue. And if the merchants likes to take a woman with him from Tana, he can do so; if he does not like to take one there is no obligation, only if he does take one he will be kept more comfortably than if he does not take one. Howbeit, if he does take one, it will be well that she be acquainted with the Cumanian tongue as well as the men . . .

The road from Tana to Cathay[7] is perfectly safe, whether by day or by night, according to what the merchants say who have used it. Only if a merchant, in going or coming, should die upon the road, everything belonging to him will become the perquisite of the lord of the country in which he dies, and the officers of the lord will take possession of all. And in a like manner if he die in Cathay. But if his brother be with him, or any intimate friend and comrade calling himself his brother, then to such a one they will surrender the property of the deceased, and so it will be rescued . . .

Cathay is a province which contains a multitude of cities and towns. Among those there is one in particular, that is to say the capital city, to which merchants flock, and in which there is a vast amount of trade; and this city is called Cambalec.[8] And the said city has a circuit of one hundred miles, and is all full of people and houses and of dwellers . . .

You may calculate that a merchant with a dragoman, and with two men servants, and with goods to the value of twenty-five thousand golden florins,[9] should spend on his way to Cathay from sixty to eighty sommi[10] of silver, and not more if he manages well; and for all the road back again from Cathay to Tana, including the expenses of living and the pay of servants, and all other charges, the cost will be about five sommi per head of pack animals, or something less. And you may reckon the sommo to be worth about five golden florins. You may reckon also that each ox-wagon will require one ox, and will carry ten cantars Genoese weight; and the camel-wagon will require three camels, and will carry thirty cantars Genoese weight; and the horse-wagon will require one horse, and will commonly carry six and a half cantars of silk, at 250 Genoese pounds[11] to the cantar. And a bale of silk may be reckoned at between 110 and 116 Genoese pounds . . .

Anyone from Genoa or from Venice, wishing to go to the places above-named, and to make the journey to Cathay, should carry linens with him, and if he visits Organci[12] he will dispose of these well. In Organci he should purchase *sommi* of silver, and with these he should proceed without making any further investment, unless it be some bales of the very finest stuffs which go in small bulk, and cost no more for carriage than course stuffs would do . . .

Whatever silver the merchants may carry with them as far as Cathay the lord of Cathay[13] will take from them and put into his treasury. And to merchants who thus bring their silver they give paper money of theirs in exchange. This is of yellow paper, stamped with the seal of the lord aforesaid. And this money is called *balishi;* and with this money you can readily buy silk and all other merchandise that you have a desire to buy. And all the people of the country are bound to receive it. And you shall not pay a higher price for your goods because your money is paper. And of the said paper money there are three kinds, one being worth more than another, according to the value which has been established for each by that lord.

Two Silken Artifacts

The following silk objects are part of the collection of London's Victoria and Albert Museum.

1) Woven Silk cloth (800–1000 C.E.)
This cloth comes from a church in the French town of Huy. It is part of a group of textiles that were found in various parts of Europe and Russia. Exactly where they came from is difficult to say. The dyes appear to be Chinese, but the decoration seems to derive from pre-Islamic Persia. On the backs of some of the pieces are inscriptions in Sogdian, and the thread is unlike silk found in other parts of Eurasia at the time in that it seems to be the product of a rather primitive spinning and weaving process (Figure 4.3).

2) Dalmatic (circa 1400 C.E.)
This dalmatic, a liturgical garment worn by deacons, was used in fifteenth-century Italy. It is made of silk and woven metal thread. The silk cloth was produced in Persia, and its decorations include Chinese

FIGURE 4.3 A silk cloth, found in a French Church, dating from the ninth or tenth centuries.

Source: V & A Picture Library.

decorative motifs, such as the phoenix, a mythical bird that originated in Ancient Egypt, was adopted by the Greco-Roman World, and reached China by way of Central Asia. The cloth, which also is emblazoned with traditional Islamic floral motifs, was then made into a dalmatic in Italy (Figure 4.4).

Both cloths were used in Christian churches. Is there anything Christian about their decoration? What do you know about the phoenix, for example, that might have made it a symbol of one of the core beliefs of Christianity? Beyond any symbolism, was there anything else that made these clothes so desirable in churches? Both derive, at least in part, from the Islamic world. What does this suggest about the relationship between Western Europe and the Islamic world that these cloths were in churches? What does it tell us that both these cloths have some elements in them that derive from China?

FIGURE 4.4 A silk dalmatic from fifteenth century Italy. Dalmatics were liturgical garments worn by deacons.

Source: V & A Picture Library.

NOTES

1. Mesopotamia, modern-day Iraq.
2. An island in the Aegean Sea.
3. China.
4. A town in the Crimea.
5. An interpreter and guide.
6. A Turkic language of central Asia.
7. North China.
8. Or Khanbalik—"City of the [Mongol] Khan." The city would later become Beijing.
9. A florin, the official coin of Florence, weighed 3.53 grams of pure (24 caret) gold.
10. The sommo (singular of sommi) was a weight of silver.
11. Genoese pound=about 12 ounces.
12. City on the Oxus River.
13. The Mongol Great Khan.

CHAPTER

Making Connections: How Much Have Things Changed?

COMMERCE CIRCA 1750

By 1750 the world was girdled by maritime trade routes. Europeans used and copied Chinese porcelain in such quantities that we still call it "china." They wore enough Indian cotton that words like "madras" and "calico," the names of Indian port cities, became standard names for varieties of cotton cloth. Europeans drank chocolate from Mexico, tea from China, and coffee from Yemen and sweetened it with sugar from the Caribbean. West Africans used guns made in Europe, cloth from North Africa and Europe, drank Dutch gin, and salted their food with Saharan salt. East Africans ate dates from the Persian Gulf, wore Indian cloth, and were every bit as fond of Chinese porcelain as the Europeans. In East Asia, China continued to import spices and luxury foods from Southeast Asia and to export silk yarn and the porcelain and lacquerware that the rest of the world so desired, all the while circulating huge quantities of goods within the vast expanse of the

Qing Empire. China and Japan both made efforts to limit and control the degree to which foreign merchants could trade with them. In China this meant limiting trade to several treaty ports and in Japan legal trade was restricted to a single island in Nagasaki harbor. But in both places there was a lively, though not risk-free, smuggling industry.

These trade systems, and by 1750 it would not be unreasonable to speak of a single, interconnected, world trade *system*, moved people along with goods. Most obviously, the sugar trade depended on the forced movement of Africans to the Americas. But others moved too. The heroine of *Moll Flanders,* an 18th-century English novel, is transported to Virginia where she works as an indentured servant in the tobacco fields, but ends up rising in Virginia society and becoming a wealthy planter. Moll may be fictitious, but many English convicts were transported to Barbados or to Virginia in lieu of hanging, where they went to work growing sugar or tobacco, and some became founders of influential families. Likewise, English, Dutch, and French merchants lived in India and Southeast Asia. The wealthy Anglo-Indian merchant is almost as common a theme in the English novel as the wealthy West Indian planter. Indian merchants lived in East Africa and the Persian Gulf. Armenian merchants lived in the cities of North India, and Chinese merchants lived in the ports of Southeast Asia.

Not only was there cross-cultural trade, there was cross-cultural industry. Some industries became symbiotic parts of a complex global network. The Massachusetts rum industry relied on imported molasses from the West Indies. In turn, the West Indian sugar industry relied on imported labor from Africa and milling equipment from Europe. What is more, trade goods were often modified locally rather than used in their original forms. West African weavers, like weavers in many other places, unraveled and rewove imported cloth to better suit local tastes. Shipyards in western India built European-style ships out of local woods for European and Indian customers. By marrying European designs with high quality woods like teak (itself often imported) and using skilled but cheap local labor, these shipyards produced some of the world's finest ships.

Trade integrated consumption, production, and labor to such an extent all over the world that people who had never seen the sea or even traveled out of their own villages made livings in ways that depended on world trade. East Africans hunted ivory so that Indian brides could wear ivory bangles. Indian peasants grew indigo that dyed woolen cloth in Europe. Even in the sub-Arctic regions of Canada and Siberia, people hunted and trapped to feed a distant market's demands for fur. To be sure, probably most workers were only tangentially affected by global trade networks before 1750, but their presence was felt all over the world.

The other crucial characteristic of this period is the relative parity among all the participants. With the notable exception of major regions of the Americas, where pre-Columbian political and social structures crumbled after their initial contact with Europeans, in Africa and Eurasia no one state or region ever had the means to dominate the others. Europeans had trading posts in Asia, but they paid market prices for what they bought. Europeans had impressive looking fortified castles on the West African Coast, but there too they saw the prices they paid for slaves rise steadily throughout the 18th century. Arguably the most extensive and wealthiest place in the world in 1750 was China, but even the Chinese had to grudgingly permit more European trade than they were happy with. The merchants of the world before 1750 lived in a world that one historian has described as a world of "compromise and accommodation," which simply means that no group of merchants had the means at hand consistently to overwhelm the others.

A Final Question

This brings us to what will be our final question. How much did things change after 1750? Is trade more important now than it was then? Is it as culturally significant now as it was then? Is the modern global economy fundamentally different from what preceded it, or does it have roots in the past? Historians do not all agree as to the answers to these questions, and, indeed, one might take the position that it is too soon to tell. But let us proceed and try to make historical sense of the tangle of commercial changes that have taken place since 1750 but with the humility to acknowledge that our answers are open to debate. You, the reader, must decide the strength or weakness of our conclusions.

Modernity

If 1750 is considered the watershed between the modern world and the pre-modern world, perhaps it is worth considering what historians mean by the term "modern." For historians, modernity is defined by a set of social, political, and economic habits. Modernity is characterized by nation-states that ideally impose a uniform legal system on all their citizens and are themselves the main actors in large-scale politics. Thus, international trade agreements are fundamentally modern in that they are predicated on agreements between nations. In a modern world, New York City cannot give preferential treatment to goods coming from Shanghai while imposing punitive tariffs on goods from Nagasaki. It is nation-states not cities, or individuals for that matter, that make these agreements.

Modern societies are also defined by institutions and bureaucracies that have supplanted the personal, face-to-face human relationships of the pre-modern world. In a modern business it is the director of shipping, who might be from Japan, who deals with to the regional sales manager, who might be a citizen of Mexico. Moreover, both might have been appointed just a week earlier, but their relationship is defined by their institutional positions. In a traditional business, people dealt with relatives and co-religionists, with family trees and shared cultures taking the place of bureaucracies.

Industrial production is also considered modern, whereas agricultural activity is associated with traditional, pre-modern societies. The factory, with its closely supervised and clock-driven work, where hourly wage-earners are cogs in a larger organizational structure, is quintessentially modern; indentured agriculture, where tenant farmers did different jobs in different seasons, and worked to seasonal rhythms—long hours in the summer, hardly at all in the winter—for a landlord who had known their family for generations defines the traditional.

Obviously these are idealized models. Institutions and bureaucracies like the Roman Catholic Church or the Chinese scholararchy long predate 1750, and it is still easier to become the regional sales manager if your cousin is the director of shipping. Some American cities try to conduct their own foreign policies (Berkeley, CA; Boulder, CO; and Burlington, VT have each made laws intended to affect nations with dodgy human rights records) and even as modern a place as the United States has fifty different state constitutions and codes of law. But in general, for the last 250 years the nation-state has been the defining legal and commercial entity in the world.

However, it now looks as though the nation-state is declining in importance, at least as far as trade goes. A number of factors seem to nibbling away at the integrity of the nation-state, which suggests that the conditions we describe as modernity may not be a permanently new set of conditions but rather a temporary deviation from historical norms.

The Age of Industry

If there is one incontestable area where change came dramatically and permanently after 1750, it is in the production of goods. The rise of industries that substituted fossil fuels for human, animal, or water power not only changed the way goods were produced, it made possible new types and quantities of goods. Shortly after 1750, the process for coke smelting of iron, once used in Song China but later forgotten, was rediscovered in England. Iron and steel were now being produced in huge quantities using coke, a specially treated coal, rather than charcoal. Soon coal-powered steam engines were being used to run factories, to power ships, and to propel trains. These changes happened in Britain first, but then spread rapidly, despite the best efforts of the British government, to other parts of Europe and to North America. But for a variety of reasons, these industries remained a virtual monopoly of the Western nations until the end of the 19th century.

That the West monopolized these technologies had important implications for world trade. First it meant that Europeans could make some products much more cheaply than others could. Cotton textiles, once almost an Indian monopoly, suddenly were being produced in vast quantities in English cities such as Manchester and New England cities like Lowell. Both places were too cold to support the growth of cotton plants, but their manufacturing processes were so efficient that it made the cost of bringing cotton to the mills irrelevant. Cotton grown in Alabama or Egypt could be shipped by rail or steam ship to mills in Lowell or Manchester and the finished product could then be put on ships and sent to India where it could compete against locally made cotton textiles.

This gave the West a commercial advantage in almost every market in the world. Even in the time when the EIC and VOC were at their most powerful in the Indian Ocean, both had been forced to engage in local trade: moving goods within the Indian Ocean in order to generate enough cash to purchase the goods they wanted to ship back to Europe. Now Europeans produced goods that let them buy whatever they wanted. Cheap European manufactured goods started to appear everywhere.

This was the beginning of what is has been dubbed "the death of distance." Transportation costs were becoming low enough that they were rarely the determining factor in setting prices. If we compare this with the sort of trade we saw in ancient times, where transportation cost were much higher, the difference is remarkable. In Pliny's time the cost of moving goods as bulky as Chinese silks and Indian cottons textiles from Asia to the Mediterranean was so high that these items were rare luxuries. By contrast, in the 19th century, cotton textiles made in the US were flooding the East African market, where they were so cheap that they were used as clothing for slaves.

As the cost of moving goods shrank, so did the cost of moving information. It is a commonplace that the internet and modern telecommunications have made the world shrink dramatically in the last 20 years, but something similar and perhaps more dramatic was going on in the 19th century. The development first of the telegraph and then of the undersea cable, meant that by 1870 it was possible to send a message from India to England and to get a response in under an hour. Seventy years earlier the same message would have take about 18 months to make the round trip journey from India to England and back again. The implications of this communications revolution for trade were dramatic—every bit as dramatic as the fall in transportation costs.

Before the telegraph, ships were dispatched to their destination without the owners of the cargo knowing what local prices for their cargo would be. A British merchant in East Africa trying to decide whether to ship a cargo of ivory to India or Britain had to guess where the prices would be best. The most recent information he might have for India would be a month out of date and several months out of date for Britain. Even if he made the right call, it was entirely possible that the arrival of a ship or two carrying the same cargo might get to port before his ship and prices would collapse. With the telegraph in place merchants could not only know prices before their goods shipped, but even as they were in transit. If prices moved after a ship left port, the captain could be sent a message to proceed to another port where prices were better. As information became cheaper, trade became less risky.

This in turn triggered a new way of doing business. Cheap and dependable transportation meant that an industry could rely on both distant markets and distant supplies of raw materials. Steamships are not necessarily faster than sailing ships but they are much more pre-dictable. An Atlantic crossing in a sailing ship might take three weeks one time and six the next. If a factory must have the cotton on that ship to keep running, that is a problem. Steamships, because they do not depend on the wind, can run to a schedule. A steamship company can announce to its customers that a ship will arrive every Thursday carrying the cotton that they need. It can also say that every Tuesday a ship will leave and it will carry away the cloth that has been made from the raw cotton. When the cotton cloth reached its market the proceeds of the sale could be wired back to the factory and used to buy more raw cotton. Thus, steamships and telegraphs were the per-fect complement to industrial production. They facilitated the inte-gration of European and North American industry with their sources of supply and with their markets.

This made industry increasingly dependent on raw materials from distant places. Most of the fibers used in European industry, such as cotton, jute, sisal, and coconut coir, came from warmer, far-distant places. Dyestuffs were also imported from the tropics. Rubber and gutta-percha (a sort of natural plastic) were harvested in the tropics. Gum copal, used to make varnish, came from East African trees. Ivory, used for many of the purposes where plastic would now be employed, also came from the tropics. This dependence on tropical raw materials occurred, not coincidentally, during the apogee of European empire.

Between 1850 and 1950 the parity among the various regions of the world that was the characteristic of the period before 1750 broke down. Using the wealth and weaponry generated by their industries, Europeans rapidly conquered most of Africa, solidified their grasp on South Asia and the Middle East, and defeated the last remaining pockets of resistance in the Americas. They used this dominance to ensure reliable supplies of raw materials and to provide protected markets for their industries. This marked a major departure from the era before 1750. A commercial world that had once contained many roughly equal participants was now slanted heavily toward the West. Not only did the West outproduce everyone else, it ruthlessly stamped out competitors. When several Indian-owned cotton plants threatened British industry in India, tariff manipulation put the Indi-ans out of business. Japan, which industrialized and managed to compete with European industry in a few arenas, was the exception.

The cultural impact of trade and empire was huge. European manufactured goods were found everywhere. European cloth, bicycles, pots and pans, kerosene lamps, blankets, books, newspapers, candles, musical instruments, and even processed foods were available virtually everywhere on the planet. With these goods came European businessmen, colonial officials, engineers, missionaries, and in some places settlers.

This era may have been different in the volume of trade and in the lopsided nature of the trade, but it was similar to earlier times in that trade goods were still culturally sticky. They brought with them people and ideas. Steamships were fast and efficient but they still needed large crews. Ports were still full of people from all over the world, rubbing shoulders and sharing news, music, ideas, and a few drinks and/or blows. European empire and trade spread western styles of dress, education, table manners, legal codes, medicine, and technology with an efficiency unmatched in earlier times.

A Twentieth-Century Turning Point?

Some historians argue that the thirty years before World War I was the most commercially open and integrated period in world history. Tariffs were low, transportation was efficient, and industry routinely relied on imported raw material and export markets. World War I brought all this to an end. European businesses that had seen their raw materials disappear as global trade collapsed during the war sought out new ways of doing business in the aftermath of the war. They lobbied for protectionist tariffs and for exclusive access to colonial markets and raw materials. The world wide depression of the 1930s exacerbated this trend, as did a further disruption of trade during the Second World War.

By 1950, the freewheeling trading world of the late 19th century was a distant memory. Average import duties were as high as 40 percent—high enough that they were prohibitive for many products. Synthetics developed during the war made industry less reliant on imported raw materials and national economies were as insular as they had been at any time in the 20th century. But in the midst of this the beginnings of a new era in global commerce were in the making.

The Age of the Shipping Container

Even before the end of World War II, planning for the world's economic recovery began. In 1944 representatives of the Allied powers met at Bretton Woods, New Hampshire and held the first of a series of meetings aimed at creating conditions favorable to world trade, in the belief that this would speed economic recovery from the war and that struggles over trade had been one of the causes of the war. The trend toward trade liberalization that began at Bretton Woods has continued into the present. Since Bretton Woods, trade tariffs have steadily dropped all over the world. The global average is less than 5 percent of the value of imports. Organizations like the World Trade Organization (WTO) are now focusing less on tariffs that on other obstacles to free trade. By way of example, subsidies, especially to agriculture in the developed world, have much the same effect as trade tariffs.

The world-wide commitment to the principle (if not always the practice) of free trade has caused an unprecedented boom in global trade. The volume and pace of world trade is staggering. There is hardly an industry left in the world that does not have to compete on a global scale. Free trade means grape growers in California have to worry about competition from Chile, Mexico, and South Africa. African rice farmers have to compete against American rice growers. A shoe factory in France relies on energy from the Middle East and leather from Senegal and has to compete against Asian factories with cheaper labor. Cars can be assembled in Canada from parts that appear simultaneously, just as they are needed, from all over the world. What makes all this possible is the humble shipping container.

The single most efficient means of moving goods is over water. Once goods are in a ship the energy and labor costs of moving them from one place to another are negligible. The hard part, and thus the expensive part, is getting them in and out of the ship. In 1956, the New York Port Authority (NYPA) employed 31,000 longshoremen, whose job it was wrestle the cargo in and out of ships. They used cranes, nets, and muscle to get the job done. Cargo was packed into the holds in units as small as the cardboard box or the bunch of bananas, each of which had to be shifted by human hands. Today, despite a significant increase in the volume of trade that passes through the NYPA, only 3,000 people are needed to handle all the cargo.

This new efficiency is the brainchild of Malcolm Mclean, the inventor the shipping container. He had been in the trucking business, and it struck him that it is horribly inefficient to unload truck trailers into warehouses, shift the contents of the warehouse into a ship, and then when the ship reaches port to shift its contents into truck trailers again. In 1954 he stripped the wheels off truck trailers, reinforced the sides so that they could be stacked, and bought a ship that he named the *Ideal X*. In 1956 his new company Sea-Land launched a service between New York and Houston, and intermodal transport (i.e. transport that can shift almost seamlessly from truck to train to ship) was born.

Initially there was resistance to containerization. Longshoremen referred to the containers as "longshoreman's coffins" because so many of their number were put out of work by them. Shipping companies did not want to invest in new types ships and cranes. The working life of a ship can be as long as 50 years, and the design of containerships is fundamentally different from other ships, so the shipping companies were hesitant to abandon proven technology to switch to an unproven and expensive technology. But over time they embraced it.

Now, 60 percent of maritime trade moves in containers. About the only goods that do not are liquids, bulk grains, and minerals, such as coal and iron ore. But clothing, electronics, and food—all mainstays of the global economy—are shipped in containers. In many ways the container shipping industry is the logistical equivalent of the internet. Each container is the equivalent of a digital packet. All are interchangeable in makeup, and each has an address on it indicating its destination. Cargo is loaded into the container at the factory, and the address is tagged to the container. It is then sent to a port, which itself functions much like a router does in the internet. In fact, people in the container business talk about "through put," the same term used in digital networks. Container through put is measured not in bytes, but in TEUs (twenty foot equivalent units). In the port the container's address indicates where it is going, and it is placed on a ship headed the right way. When that ship arrives at port the container is routed onto another ship or train or truck. No one actually touches the cargo between when the container is loaded at the factory and when it is unloaded at its final destination.

The small amount of handling that the containers require is done by huge cranes. The cranes require real skill of their operators, but one person can do the work that formerly required dozens if not hundreds of longshoremen. At one port in Germany human truck drivers have been replaced by automated trucks that shuttle containers through the port. Containerships themselves can carry huge amounts of cargo, but have tiny crews. So much of their operation is automated, there is just not that much need for people on them. The result is a huge drop in the cost of shipping. Transport costs are so low that less than 1 percent of the cost of finished goods is transportation cost. The death of distance that began with steamships has reached its culmination with the containership. The economies of scale that containerships produce are such that it can be cheaper to ship goods from Hong Kong to Los Angeles than from Los Angeles to St. Louis.

So, more than ever before, commerce thrives. One historian has pointed out that the entire trade of the Indian Ocean in any given year of the 17th century could be carried in a single modern containership. But are the high volumes of trade as culturally significant as the lesser volumes of trade were in earlier periods? Certainly ports cities are not the cultural melting pots they once were. In the age of sail, ships needed large crews in relation to their size. Thus, every ton or so of cargo that moved across the water was accompanied by a person. In the age of the steamship, that ratio dropped, but there were still significant numbers of sailors needed run a ship. Ports were lively places (Cape Town, South Africa was known as the Tavern of the Seven Seas), mostly because of the large population of transient sailors. By contrast, the modern container port is a virtual desert. There are few longshoremen and fewer sailors. Trade goods bring many fewer people with them than they once did.

The other cultural result of containerization is that it has broken down the boundaries of regional trade systems. Before 1750 there was an Indian Ocean World, created and maintained by trade within the bounds of that ocean. Some goods crossed the boundaries between the Atlantic and the Indian Ocean and some between the Pacific and the Indian Ocean, but the cost of long-distance transportation was enough to limit these flows. Seas and oceans, such as the Mediterranean, the Atlantic, and the Indian Ocean, were distinct commercial places with their own goods and commercial traditions. The same could be said for the Sahara or the Central Asian deserts. Now, because shipping containers slip so easily across the boundaries that once defined these separate worlds, it is harder to see the oceans as separate commercial worlds. From a commercial perspective, there is just one big Ocean and even the boundaries between it and the land are fuzzy. As a shipping company executive said recently, "All the romance has gone out of the business."

Contemporary Information Technology

The contemporary analogues of the telegraph—modern telecommunications and the internet—seem to have usurped the cultural role once played by trade. The death of distance that has characterized logistics has also reshaped communications. It costs no more to send an e-mail across oceans than it does across town. International long distance telephony is now cheaper than long distance calling was within the US twenty years ago, and international rates continue to drop. As a result, cross-cultural interaction is more likely to take place over a phone or computer terminal than on the wharfs.

Perhaps the most interesting indication of this shift is the effort of many nations to control the internet. China, which has wholeheartedly embraced international trade, is still quite leery of information technology. The "Great Firewall of China" (as it is known in the West) is the Chinese government's effort to block certain web sites that it wishes to prevent its citizens from reading. At various times, even search engines, such as Yahoo and Google, have been blocked in China. Similar filtering efforts have been employed in various parts of the Middle East, where governments wish to get the economic benefits of information but fear the cultural influence that come with the internet. The barbarians used to show up in treaty ports; now they are in your inbox. It is fair to ask: Were efforts by some regimes to control the influx of foreign ideas and culture along with the trade goods that traveled with them effective in the past? Can similar efforts today to control or prevent the passage of foreign ideas along electronic avenues succeed?

So how much have things changed? Somehow wearing sneakers made in Malaysia does not seems as culturally charged as wearing imported silk once was. Porcelain was called "china," but no one calls sneakers "malaysia." But culture that flows through wires is crossing borders at a furious rate. Twenty years ago no one would have dreamed that American children would be watching J-pop stars on television. *Hi Hi Puffy AmiYumi* anyone?

Bibliography

Useful Works on Pre-Modern Trade and Commerce

Phillip Curtin, *Cross-Cultural Trade in World History* (1984) is the place to start for a world history of trade. Its main failing is that it stops in the nineteenth century. Arjun Appadurai, ed., *Social Life of Things: Commodities in Social Perspective* (1988) is a collection of articles by anthropologists about the way commodities have been treated by various societies. Fernand Braudel, *The Wheels of Commerce: Civilization and Capitalism* (1983) is a vast and far-reaching study of early modern commerce. "Magisterial" almost seems like an under-statement for this book. It is European oriented but includes some Asian material. K.N. Chaudhuri, *Asia before Europe* (1991) is a challenging book. In the preface, the author advises readers not inter-ested in theory to skip certain chapters. Heed his advice. That said, this is an interesting and useful attempt to do for Asia what Braudel did for Europe. Patricia Risso, *Merchants and Faith* (1995) is a short and accessible work that looks at the role of Islam in the trade of the Indian Ocean. Robert Lopez, *Commercial Revolution of the Middle Ages*

(1976) provides a survey of trade in medieval Europe. Kenneth Pommeranz and Steven Topik, *The World the Trade Created* (2000) is a collection of short articles the authors wrote for a business magazine. Here one can find lots of interesting stories about surprising commodities, such as guano. C.G.F. Simkin, *Traditional Trade of Asia* (1968) is a survey of Asian trade without the Braudelian ambitions of Chaudhuri's work. James Tracey, ed., *Rise of Merchant Empires: Long Distance Trade in the Early Modern World* (1993) is a collection of articles that mostly focuses on Europeans in the early modern commercial world. It is especially good on the Chartered Companies.

Useful Works on Spice

On the spice trade in the ancient world James Miller, *The Spice Trade of the Roman Empire* (1969) is the standard work. It includes the most complete analysis of the terms used by ancient writers to refer to spices, as well as a historical overview of the ancient spice trade. For a more recent, and broader overview of the spice trade, Andrew Dalby, *Dangerous Tastes* (2002) makes a good starting place. For a broad overview of the Indian Ocean world the best place to start is K.N. Chaudhuri, *Trade and Civilization in the Indian Ocean* (1985). More recently, Michael Pearson has written a thought provoking general history, *World of the Indian Ocean* (2005). For spices as foods nothing compares with Harold McGee's recently updated classic, *On Food and Cooking*. Also of interest in this vein is Felipe Fernandez-Armesto, *Near a Thousand Tables* (2002) possibly the most interesting history of food yet written. For the age of the European Companies, see C.R. Boxer, *Portuguese Seaborne Empire* (1969) and *Dutch Seaborne Empire* (1980). More recently Rene Barendse, *Arabian Seas* offers a finely textured look at the commercial world of the Indian Ocean in the seventeenth century, but it can be a challenging read.

Useful Works on Salt

There are remarkably few English-language treatments of salt in history that are accessible to the general reader. The most approachable is Mark Kurlansky, *Salt: A World History* (2003). S.A.M. Adshead, *Salt and Civilization* (1992) and Robert Multhauf, *Neptune's Gift: A History of Common Salt* (1978) provide a somewhat more in-depth introduction to salt production, trade, and government regulation. Approachable surveys in English of salt in the context of Chinese history are particularly rare. Kwan Man Bun, *Salt Merchants of Tianjin: State Making and Civil Society in Late Imperial China* (2001) is an exception to the rule. For West Africa, students and general readers are lucky to have Paul Lovejoy, *Salt of the Desert Sun: A History of Salt Production and Trade in the Central Sudan* (1986). For general information regarding Chinese history, see Albert M. Craig, *The Heritage of Chinese Civilization* (2000) or Patricia Ebrey, *Cambridge Illustrated History of China* (1999). For a general introduction to African History, see Erik Gilbert and Jonathan T. Reynolds, *Africa in World History* (2004) or Phyllis Martin and Patrick O'Meara, *Africa* (1995).

Useful Works on Sugar

If you wish to read just one book about sugar, it should be Sidney Mintz, *Sweetness and Power* (1985) which offers an intriguing look at the history of sugar consumption and production. Mintz is an anthropologist, so the book is organized in ways that might seem alien to the historian, but the result is fascinating and thought provoking. For a more traditional look at the history of sugar, a collection of essays by Phillip Curtin, *Rise and Fall of the Plantation Complex* (1998) is the best place to start. On the cultural impact of the sugar and slave trades see, John Thornton's *Africa and Africans in the Making of the Atlantic World* (1998). Also in this vein see David Eltis, *Rise of African Slavery in the Americas* (1999). For arguments surrounding the economic role of the plantation complex see David Landes, *The Wealth and Poverty of Nations* (1999).

Useful Works on Silk

The best place to start is the recent update of Luce Boulnois' magisterial *Silk Road: Monks, Warriors, and Merchants on the Silk Road* (2004). In addition to a narrative history of the silk road, this book has maps, pictures, and a historical gazetteer that tells the modern locations and equivalents of ancient place names. It even has an appendix that offers advice on how to travel the Silk Road. Buy this one. Other interesting books on the Silk Road's role as a conduit for cross-cultural interchange include Jonathan Tucker, *The Silk Road: Art and History* (2003) and Frances Wood, *The Silk Road: Two Thousand Years in the Heart of Asia* (2002). For a treatment of silk in China, see Shelagh Vainker's lavishly illustrated *Chinese Silk: A Cultural History* (2004).

For religious change and exchange on the Silk Road, see Richard Foltz, *Religions of the Silk Road* (2000). To follow the route of a Buddhist pilgrim on the Silk Road, see Sally Wriggins, *The Silk Road Journey with Xuanzang*, revised and updated (2003). For a look at the history of the rediscovery of the Silk Road, see Peter Hopkirk, *Foreign Devils on the Silk Road* (1984). For the silk trade in the Islamic world, see Rudolph Matthee, *Politics of Trade in Safavid Iran: Silk for Silver* (1999). Also worth a look are www.silk-road.com and www.silkroadproject.org.

DOCUMENT SOURCES

Spice Documents

Pliny, *Natural History*, Book XII, H. Rackham, trans., vol. IV, Loeb Classical Library (Cambridge, MA, Harvard University Press: 2000) pp. 19–21, 63–69.

Letter from Khalaf b. Issac to Abraham b. Yiju is from S.D. Goiten, *Letters of Medieval Jewish Traders* (Princeton, NJ, Princeton University Press: 1973) pp. 187–191.

Duarte Barbosa, *The Book of Duarte Barbosa*, vol. I, Mansel Longworth Dames, trans. and ed. (London, Hakluyt: 1918) pp. 53–58.

Garcia da Orta, *Colloquies in the Simples and Drugs of India: Cinnamon, Cloves, Mace and Nutmeg and Pepper*, Sir Clements Markham trans. and ed. (London, Henry Sotheran: 1913) pp. 118–128, 367–373.

Salt Documents

Discourse on Salt and Iron: A Debate on State Control of Commerce and Industry in Ancient China, Translation by Esson M. Gale from original text by Huan K' uan. E.J. Brill, Leiden, 1931, *Journal of the North China Branch of the Royal Asiatic Society*, pp. 85–91.

Aobo Tu, from *Salt Production Techniques in Ancient China, The Aobo Tu.* Translated from Chinese by Yoshida Tora, translated and revised by Hans Ulrich Vogel. E.J. Brill, Leiden: 1993, pp. 121–149.

al-Bakri, from N. Levtzion and J.F.P. Hopkins, eds, *Corpus of Early Arabic Sources for West African History* (Princeton, NJ: 2000) pp. 69–82.

Ibn Battuta, from N. Levtzion and J.F.P. Hopkins, eds, *Corpus of Early Arabic Sources for West African History* (Princeton, NJ: 2000) pp. 282–287.

Sugar Documents

Gomes Eannes de Azurara, *The Chronicle of the Discovery and Conquest of Guinea*, vol. 1, Charles Beazley trans. (London: Hakluyt: 1896) pp. 27–31.

Richard Ligon, *A True and Exact History of the Island of Barbadoes, 1657,* reprint (London, Frank Cass: 1970) pp. 46, 86, 96.

George Warren, *An Impartial Description of Surinam* (London, Godbid: 1667) in microfilm, Wing: Early English Books, STC II, Year 13, Reel 480, pp. 18–20.

Thomas Phillips, *Journal of a Voyage Made in the Hannibal 1693–4* (London, Lintot: 1746) in microfiche [Early Exploration and Discovery] LAC 400045 card A6, pp. 234–235, 248, 252.

Sources for Silk Documents

Pliny Book XI is from Pliny, *Natural History,* Books VIII–XI, H. Rackham, trans. Vol. III, Loeb Classical Library (Cambridge, MA, Harvard University Press: 1997) pp. 231–233, 477–481.

Xuanzang excerpt is from Hiun Tsiang, *Si-Yu-Ki, Buddhist Records of the Western World,* Samuel Beal, trans. (London: Kegan Paul, Trench, Tubener, Paragon Book Reprint: 1968) pp. 318–319.

Pegolotti is taken from Henry Yule and Henri Cordier, trans. and eds, *Cathay and the Way Thither* (London, Hakluyt: 1916) pp. 143–171.

Index